You Want to Pierce What?

You Want to Pierce What?

Getting a Grip on Today's Family

Walker Moore

Marshall Pickering
An Imprint of HarperCollins*Publishers*

Marshall Pickering is an Imprint of
HarperCollins*Religious*
Part of HarperCollins*Publishers*
77–85 Fulham Palace Road, London W6 8JB

First published in 1997 by Albury Publishing, Tulsa, Oklahoma
This edition 1998 published by HarperCollins*Publishers*

Available in other languages from Access Sales International (ASI)
2448 E. 81st Street, Ste. 4705, Tulsa, OK 74137, USA. Fax number 918 496 2822

1 3 5 7 9 10 8 6 4 2

A catalogue record for this book is
available from the British Library

ISBN 0 551 03177 8

Unless otherwise indicated, all Scripture quotations are taken from the *King James Version* of the Bible.

Printed and bound in Great Britain by
Caledonian International Book Manufacturing Ltd, Glasgow

I dedicate this book to my mother, Katie Lou Moore, who spent her entire life loving children.

Even on the last day of her life, she spent it telling boys and girls in a children's home about Jesus.

To my wife, Cathy, who is the finest mother any two boys could have. She is the best helpmate any husband could ever be blessed with.

To my sons, Jeremiah and Caleb, who are the joy of my life, and without their stories this book could not be written.

To Lucile Hodges, who encouraged me to go for my dream and has been beside me the entire time.

To so many who have suffered along with me in writing this book. Shelly Tipps, who helped come up with the title. Chris Gardner, Lisa Tresch, Randy Graham, and Tom Hufty, who typed, retyped, critiqued and challenged me to make this book the best that it could be. To Tom Winters, whom God sent into my life to encourage me to put on paper the things that I had been preaching across the USA. Thanks to the wonderful staff at Albury Publishing –Pat Judd, Vicki Edwards, Jadell Forman – and a host of others who were so encouraging and patient with me during the labouring over this book.

And to our Lord and Saviour, Jesus Christ, the Head of the Church and our family. May this book bring honour and glory to You!

Contents

Part IV

You Want to Pierce What?

Getting a Grip on Communicating With Your Child

Preface

It was 1.00 a.m. on Saturday morning, a full hour past Jason's curfew. His father, Tom, watched the wall clock intensely while his mother, Carolyn, stared out of the front window. Her arms were folded and she rocked nervously back and forth on her heels.

Their eyes had met several times in the past sixty minutes, but no words were exchanged. They were each lost in thought, balancing anger with worry, fear with disbelief.

For seventeen years they had been weathering the storms of childrearing. From nappies to tricycles, to footballs to car keys, and now curfews. Unspoken questions began to shout at them from the hidden corners of their minds: 'Where is he?' 'Why doesn't he call?' 'Who is he with?' 'Is he hurt?' 'Is he dead?' 'Where did we go wrong?' It seemed as if all the years of parenting had come down to this moment.

Headlights appeared ... then passed. Carolyn turned round and Tom saw the tears in her eyes. 'Do you think he's all right?' she asked. Tom looked across the room at a picture of Jason smiling a toothless seven-year-old smile.

'I don't know,' he said.

Families today are struggling. Society has changed so dramatically that parents, even Christian parents, still feel as if they are fighting a never-ending battle. We're worried that we no longer have a grip on how to raise our children to be God-honouring men and women. Like Tom and Carolyn, we are left to wonder if our children will be all right once we release them into the world.

After twenty-five years of working with young people, I sometimes feel as if I've seen it all. But the society we live in is changing rapidly, and we have yet to see the myriad challenges that families will face in the future. The teenagers I work with now are different from the teenagers of twenty-five years ago. They have more choices, more temptations and more stress than ever before. Even primary school children are faced with pressures to do with smoking, drugs and alcohol!

Children in today's society are in danger of becoming a 'lost generation' – a generation with no values – unless the family takes seriously its role of training children to be responsible and well-rounded adults. Unfortunately, many families are not equipped to face this challenge.

Many parents are panicked, confused and desperate for a place to turn for answers. I have been there. I have cringed at the thought of releasing my precious children into a frightening world. And when the time came to release our oldest, I prayed for strength and entrusted him to the Lord. But I still cringe every now and then.

I wrote this book drawing on my experiences as a youth pastor and as a parent. During my years of working with teenagers, my wife and I were also busy with the challenges and struggles of raising our own children. When our boys were born, no one gave us the owner's manual or an instruction book on raising successful and happy children. So much of what we learned God taught us along the way, sometimes painfully. Countless times we have turned to His Word to guide us step by step and then prayed for the wisdom to carry out those truths.

This book is not an owner's manual or an instruction book. It is a book that will help you get a firm grip on what your children are facing in the world, and how you can help prepare them for it. It will give you the tools you need to build your self-confidence as a parent, and the resources to help your children become responsible, confident, and faith-filled adults. Raising children and strengthening families takes hard work, long hours, much wisdom and lots of prayer. The key is knowing the source of inspiration, patience, wisdom and guidance. God has given us His Word, the Bible, to help guide families like yours and mine. This book will help you 'get a grip' on some of what Scripture has to say about raising your children.

I have structured the book in four parts that deal with areas I have found to be stumbling blocks for families today: building self-esteem, teaching values and responsibilities, understanding escalating sexuality, and learning to communicate with each other. Among the things you will learn are ways to avoid playing the 'power game' with your teenager, why your child needs a rite of passage, and how to relieve the stress over dating. And have you heard that sexual education for seven-year-olds is wrong? I'll give you another side to the story. And because parents are not helped by theories alone, I have included practical advice at the end of each section that will help you climb over each of the four stumbling blocks.

Every parent wonders what will happen when the time comes to release their child into the world. Like Tom and Carolyn, we will all stand at the door, waiting to see if all the hard work paid off. But God promises that His wisdom is ours for the asking. So let's begin our journey together as we seek to 'get a grip' on our families.

Part I

Why Are My Children Far From Normal?

Getting a Grip on Two Things That Are Missing in Every Child's Life

Chapter 1

Rite or Wrong?

Entering the crowded fast-food restaurant, my mouth dry from the dusty air and my stomach growling for a midday meal, I looked for an empty table and immediately spotted an empty corner booth. I quickly ordered my lunch and hurried back to the staked-out booth with the food sliding back and forth across the tray. Tables around me were filled with the lunchtime crowd: a harried mother and her three energetic children, an old man with a newspaper in one hand and a half-eaten sandwich in the other, two men in business suits talking loudly with their food untouched on the table.

Suddenly out of the corner of my eye, I saw them! They were sitting facing each other with their noses almost touching, holding hands across the table and playfully feeding one another chips. They were teenagers with fresh faces and bright eyes, and they were looking at each other as if there were no one else in the room. I quickly put my drink down and leaned forward to get a closer look at them, not believing my eyes: each of the teenagers carried a machine gun slung over one shoulder!

Fear gripped my heart, and my first thought was to warn someone about these two armed teenagers. However, no one else seemed bothered by them so I began to relax again. This is Israel, I reminded myself, a country where the soldiers carry no blanks, only fully loaded, ready-to-fire guns. These were Israeli soldiers. But, they were also children.

I sat in the restaurant longer than I should have done, watching them and wondering what my reaction would have been if I were back home in the United States. How many teenagers would I trust to carry around a fully loaded machine gun out in a public place? How many would you trust? In the US, many young people have to go through a metal detector before they enter their schools to keep them from bringing in fully loaded weapons. We assume they cannot be trusted with guns. But in Israel, these two young people were already living with the realities and responsibilities of adulthood, while in the US and many other countries the assumption of adult tasks and responsibilities is often delayed as long as possible. This delay leaves mature adults frustrated and young people confused.

Parents and teachers tell numerous stories about the headaches of dealing with their children and pupils. Young people in today's society are often described as rude, lazy and apathetic. Today, there is no such thing as a 'normal' teenager. There are not many families like the ones depicted on old TV family sagas. A child's formative years used to be spent in an environment filled with everything they needed to learn the skills and acquire the knowledge to live a productive life. They were provided with a set of parents and grandparents who raised them in a loving and safe environment; nurturing families gave them the time and space to explore their potential; opportunities abounded to help them develop life skills. And they grew up *more* protected from a *less* hostile and evil world than the one children face today. Innocence was natural and biblical values expected and admired.

Times have certainly changed. Garbage isn't taken out any more, it's turned on with the click of a remote control. 'Pot' is no longer simply a place where you go for a bowel movement, and 'hip' isn't just a part of the body. And forget 'cool' if you're only talking about the temperature. Today, we have e-mail, faxes, bytes, CDs and HIV. It's no surprise that many look at the young people today and wonder, Why is this generation of children so far from normal?

Jesus Leaving His Childhood Behind

Two thousand years ago, a certain young mother was also dealing with a parenting problem. Her name was Mary.

> Every year, his [Jesus'] parents went to Jerusalem for the Feast of the Passover. When he was twelve years old, they went up to the Feast, according to the custom. After the Feast was over, while his parents were returning home, the boy Jesus stayed behind in Jerusalem, but they were unaware of it.
>
> (Luke 2:41–3 NIV)

Mary, the mother of Jesus, and her husband, Joseph, have come to Jerusalem, the largest city in the world. They have come, along with Jesus, to attend the most important of the three annual Jewish festivals, the Feast of the Passover. Biblical scholars estimate that during this era, approximately two and a half million people would have crowded into the city of Jerusalem for this holy festival.

As the story unfolds, Luke describes the sea of pilgrims travelling back to their homes. It was customary in that day for groups to travel in caravans with the women and children in front and the men behind. Since Mary and Joseph would have been walking in separate groups, they each could easily have assumed that Jesus was with the other parent.

Picture the scene: Mary has already walked a day's journey with the other women, confident her son is with the men who are walking at the back. She and the other women have been talking and sharing the experiences of the past week. The talk is animated at times, at other times they walk silently. Mary is completely unaware that her son is not a part of the caravan. The word *unaware* is important, because it tells us that Jesus did not inform His parents that He was staying behind in Jerusalem. Mary is not prone to think the worst of her son. He has never given them any trouble, so why should the thought even cross her mind that He never left the city to return home with them?

They continued to travel, but near the end of the day something inside Mary causes her to be alarmed about her son, whom she has not seen during the entire trip. With her eyes she searches the crowd stretched out behind her as they continue walking, resisting the nagging feeling that she should go and find Jesus. She expresses her concern to the women around her, but they assure her that Jesus is with the men. But Mary, being His mother, knows something is not right. An indescribable sense of panic washes over her, and rushing down the dusty road to the group of trailing men she asks if Jesus is with them. With confused looks, they shake their heads as Joseph, coming through the crowd, answers, 'I thought He was with you.'

Every parent can relate to Mary's desperation as she then goes from person to person asking, 'Have you seen my son, Jesus?' Her eyes must have been darting back and forth from person to person as she strained to see the familiar face of her special child. I know how Mary must have felt.

Once I lost my son, Caleb, in a crowded shop when he was only five years old. One minute he was next to me, the next instant he was gone. For a brief moment I was annoyed, and assumed he had only wandered away from my immediate view. But after searching for him unsuccessfully for a few short minutes, a panicky feeling made my heart pound and my palms sweat as I began running through the shop shouting his name. I asked everybody within shouting distance if they had seen my son and watched in horror as they shook their heads.

Strangely, I was reminded of Mary's dilemma again one afternoon as I stood in a bookshop staring at the pages of a book called *Where's Waldo?* For me, this is an immensely frustrating book. Hundreds of tiny people are drawn crowded on to a single page and you must find one person, named Waldo, who is hidden among the masses of cartoon humanity. I can stare at this page for twenty minutes and not be able to find him, but inevitably a little child will sneak up behind me and point him out in five seconds.

I am sure Mary wished that one of Jesus' young friends would tap her on the arm and say, 'Look, there He is, right in front of you,

you just weren't looking in the right place.' But it didn't happen. No one rescued her from her dizzying search and she continued turning in circles as she surveyed the crowd of faces, none of them her son's. Mary and Joseph decide then to return to Jerusalem, but they would have to wait until the light of the following day. I can imagine the sleepless night, Mary's prayer, and God's response, 'You lost *who?*'

Early the next morning the two of them began walking back alone to Jerusalem, terrified that they may have lost their son for ever. When they reached the still-crowded city, they continued their hunt for Jesus. The passage tells us that He was lost for three days, and on the third day Mary and Joseph, exhausted and almost without hope, finally locate Him in the temple where He is listening attentively to the learned teachers.

> After three days they found him in the temple courts, sitting among the teachers, listening to them and asking them questions. Everyone who heard him was amazed at his understanding and his answers. When his parents saw him, they were astonished. His mother said to him, 'Son, why have you treated us like this? Your father and I have been anxiously searching for you.'
>
> 'Why were you searching for me?' he asked. 'Didn't you know I had to be in my Father's house?' But they did not understand what he was saying to them.
>
> (Luke 2:46–50 NIV)

I can picture Mary with tears of joy pouring down both cheeks as she runs to embrace her son, overwhelmingly relieved that He is safe. She holds Him tighter than she ever has before as she asks Him, 'Why have you treated us this way? We've spent days worrying and looking everywhere for you!' And alongside is Joseph, repeating the line he heard as a child from his own father, 'Son, your mother and I have been worried sick about you!'

Jesus responds, 'Why? You should have known where to find Me. You should have known I would be here in My Father's house, busy with His work.'

Stop the scenario here and allow yourself to ponder how this response would be received in your house. How would you react if your child came home at 5.00 a.m. one morning, having missed the previous night's curfew by six hours? You have been calling everyone you know, even a few people you don't know, and you've spent part of the evening driving the main roads and back streets of your town. You are beyond panic and into hysteria.

Then, at 5.01 a.m., your teenager strolls in with his jacket slung over his shoulder and a calm, peaceful smile on his face. He looks at you and simply says, 'Hello.' You go crazy! After you have finished ranting and raving, he puts a hand on your shoulder and says, 'I was with my prayer group in the basement of the church. You should have known that's where I would be, why didn't you look for me there?' Would this work in your house? I don't think so.

Jesus did not hesitate in His response to Mary and Joseph. I can almost hear His voice in this passage, strong and confident, but a little surprised that it took them this long to find Him.

This story brings to mind several questions that people often ask about Jesus, the most obvious one being, Why wasn't it a sin for Jesus to stay behind in Jerusalem without telling His parents? When your child comes in past the curfew time and doesn't tell you where he has been or why he is late, it is a sin.

I've heard many people try to explain why Jesus' actions were not sinful. Some say it's because it was simply impossible for the Messiah to do anything wrong. Whatever His actions, they were always right and perfect, even if they didn't seem to make sense. Others say that Jesus was obeying his real Father instead of His earthly father. Some say Mary and Joseph were at fault. They should have kept up with Him and made sure He was present in the caravan before the journey started.

It's always easy to blame it on the parents, isn't it? But Jesus knew the Commandments. They were in His heart, including the one that says, 'Honour your father and your mother, so that you may live long in the land the Lord your God is giving you' (Exodus 20:12 NIV).

Luke's account of Jesus in the temple is significant because it marks the time in Jesus' life when He was passing from childhood into adulthood. 'And His parents used to go to Jerusalem every year at the Feast of the Passover. And when He became twelve, they went up there according to the custom of the Feast' (Luke 2:41–2 NASB). For the last eleven years, Jesus has remained behind in Nazareth as a child. Now that He is entering into adulthood, He, along with the other adults, has to attend the Feast of the Passover. He went to Jerusalem, not as a child, but as an adult. Jesus was fulfilling His adult responsibility in being obedient to His heavenly Father, and as we know from the Scriptures, this was the ultimate priority in His life. It stood above everything and everyone else. He chose that day to fulfil His responsibility to His heavenly Father, therefore His actions were not sinful.

Why was it not a sin? He did not stay behind as a child, He stayed behind as an adult. As an adult, one makes adult choices, such as whether or not to stay in a city an extra day to take care of important responsibilities. With adult choices, come adult consequences. Where did Jesus sleep for three days? Where did He eat? We do not know these answers, but we know He had to make those adult decisions.

In the first century the line separating childhood from adulthood was clear. In the Jewish custom of that day there were four great occasions that marked the progress of life: birth, maturity, marriage and death. Jesus knew that, and He knew when His childhood was over even though He continued to submit to the authority of His earthly parents. He knew when it was time to begin taking on adult responsibilities.

I think I know how Mary must have felt, having experienced similar astonishment that day I sat in the Israeli fast-food restaurant. That amazement stems from the realization that a child has become an adult and has taken on adult responsibilities. And although Jesus was no ordinary child, He and the teenage soldiers I observed shared something in common: they had all gone through a rite of passage. A rite of passage serves as an orderly way to help usher a child from one stage of his or her life into the next. It brings with it the assumption of adult responsibilities, a personal value system and the development of personal identity.

Jewish families are given specific responsibilities for educating their children. On his thirteenth birthday, a Jewish boy will participate in a 'bar mitzvah' as his formal rite of passage into adulthood. Modern-day Jewish custom provides a similar rite for girls at the age of twelve, called a 'bat mitzvah'. The young person is called on to read a prophetic passage from Scripture to the synagogue congregation. Because the young person has studied the Torah and been presented in the temple, he or she becomes a 'son or daughter of the covenant'. From that day forward, a Jewish young person is recognized as fully responsible for his or her own religious and moral actions. So the young Jewish soldiers who sat across from me that day had been recognized by their culture as adults, and they had now taken on adult responsibilities.

When Do Children Become Adults?

Although at one time in His life Jesus was a teenager, He never went through the indistinct confusion of adolescence. He never had a period of time when He was hanging in the balance between childhood and adulthood as so many children do today. In the Jewish world of Jesus' day, there were children and there were adults. The following Diagram 1 illustrates the line that separated childhood and adulthood in the Israel of Jesus' youth. In between these stages of childhood and adulthood, the child experienced a rite of passage. Today, as Diagram 2 shows, we have created an overlapping 'grey area' of life known as adolescence, when young people are neither fully child nor fully adult, but caught in between. Adolescence is a confusing time for many reasons. Some time during the late pre-teen or early teenage years hormones begin changing rapidly and rage through the body, often causing tremendous physical and emotional upheavals. These hormones cause young people to feel like adults

Diagram 1

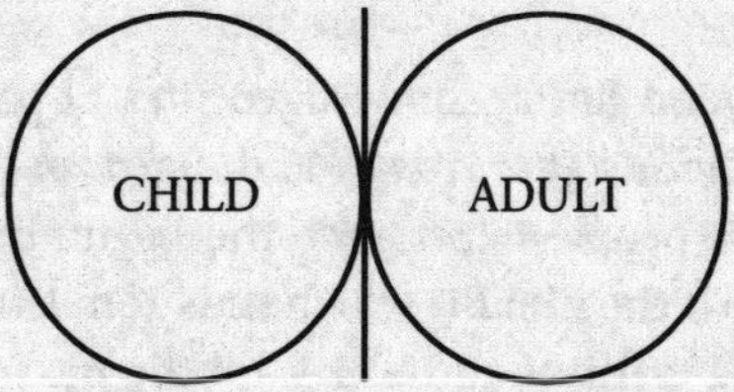

Rite of passage in the Jewish world of Jesus' day

Diagram 2

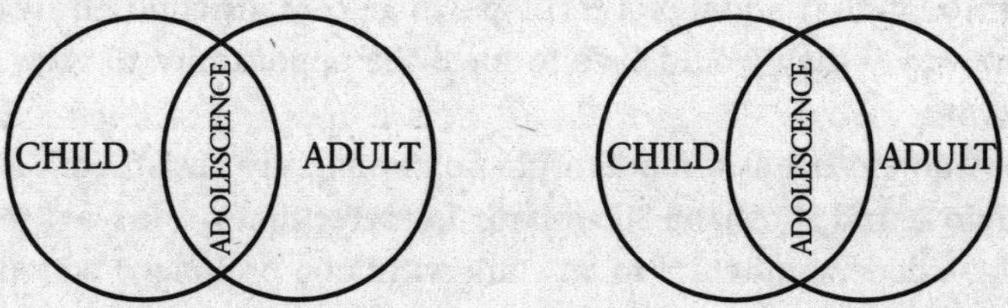

1940s: 13–18 years   Today: 9–24 years

and children at the same time. It is a stage that may sometimes start when a person is nine and not end until they are twenty-five.

Adolescence usually begins with the onset of sexual development and ends when the person has assumed complete responsibility for his or her own life. Children are beginning puberty earlier, but delaying their maturity. They are now developing sexually between the ages of eight and nine, yet they are still depending on Mum and Dad to take care of their basic needs when they leave college years later. Hence this overlap that we call adolescence continues to enlarge, resulting in a growing number of 'adult adolescents' who do not want to let go of childhood, or do not know how.

Is there something missing from the lives of our young people? Yes. Our children are missing a rite of passage which is a significant event that marks the beginning of adulthood, or the passage into adulthood.

Even Hollywood has acknowledged rites of passage. Films like *Rebel Without a Cause, Little Women* and *American Graffiti* give vivid examples of how people experience the beginning of adulthood. Another example is the film *Big* which stars Tom Hanks as a boy who makes a wish at a carnival and wakes up the next morning to find his wish has come true – his body is all grown up. The film is enthralling because we follow the challenges of a boy who has the mind of a twelve-year-old and the body of a thirty-year-old. We laugh as we see him struggle to cope in his adult body. In the end, however, he realizes he must get his twelve-year-old body back and go through the natural process of growing up. Many children are the same way – they would love to have the opportunity to grow up instantly.

'Adolescence is a modern phenomenon,' say Jewish educators Melvin L. and Shoshana Silberman. 'In earlier times, one went from being a dependent child to an adult without a prolonged period of transition. Today young people find themselves for a stretch of five years or more, as lyrics from *A Chorus Line* put it "too young to take over, too old to ignore." While they are waiting, they in effect remake their personalities, shedding childlike characteristics and trying more adult ones on for size.'[1]

At what age do children really cross over into adulthood? At seventeen you can get a driving licence, so perhaps this is the age of adulthood. Maybe, but that's in the UK. American teenagers get to drive at sixteen. But you have to wait until you are eighteen to vote or drink. Twenty-one is often seen as a highly significant birthday. So is that really the age of adulthood? Not according to the car rental companies, some of whom require you to be twenty-five to rent a car! To make this area even more confusing, in the States the government now requires you to verify that you are at least twenty-seven in order to buy cigarettes.

Restaurants, though, seem to be clear on this issue of adulthood. When I am eating out I will often ask the waitress for an 'adolescent menu' just for fun. 'You see, my son is not really a child any more, but he is not an adult either.' To date, no waitress has ever offered me an adolescent menu. In most restaurants a clear message is sent to twelve-year-olds, 'From this day forward, in our restaurant, you are now an adult!' Which, of course, means that you, as the parents, get to pay adult prices for your children to eat out.

Reading the dosage on a medicine bottle also gives us a clear definition of when the child becomes an adult. For children under twelve, one tablet; for adults of twelve and older, two tablets. There is no adolescent dosage, so when taking most medicines, you are either a child or an adult.

The point is that no one is certain when the children in our society become adults. One teenager put it this way, 'I don't know when I become an adult. First they tell me to find myself, then they tell me to get lost. I don't know which way to go!'

Advertisers seem to confuse the issue even further by using mixed images of childhood and adulthood to sell products. Children are dressed in sexy clothes and strike provocative poses to sell jeans to adults. Or, with an image appealing to children, a cartoon character is used to sell an adult product, cigarettes.

Why is the uncertainty a problem? Because the teenagers are caught in this undefined stage we call adolescence. It is as if they are trapped in a black hole not knowing when or how they will get out. In an effort to escape this abyss, young people often try to find their adulthood by using foul language, cigarettes, alcohol, drugs and sex. They think that if they participate in enough so-called adult activities, they will look at themselves or be looked at by others as an adult. Unfortunately, while they may physically appear to be adults, emotionally and mentally they are not.

Many parents tell me their adult children are moving back home, unable to cope with the realities and responsibilities of life on their own. It is a phenomenon known as 'adult adolescence'. Now they are back home, maybe back in their childhood bedroom, still reaching for the elusive adulthood, but not knowing where or how to draw the line on their childhood. These adult adolescents were out in the world, searching for ways to be adults, but took the wrong roads and messed up their lives.

My friend Mark was a young man who was always in trouble at school. His parents, however, always came to his defence. They stood up for him and blamed the school for every mess he got into. And they were always there to rescue him from the messes. His first term at college was an academic disaster. His parents, however, still blamed the college. Their son, they claimed, had not been treated fairly. When his cheques bounced they never questioned his spending habits, but simply deposited more money into his account. Mark met a girl, married her, and got a job.

Within a few months, however, he lost his job and Mum and Dad began to pay the bills for the newlyweds. The marriage began to crumble, and when the divorce was final, Mark moved back in with his parents and they continued to take care of him. At thirty-two, Mark has every need taken care of by his parents. The sad thing is, Mark enjoys it and shows no signs of wanting to be on his own as a responsible adult.

Searching for Adulthood in the Wrong Places

Children are longing for rites of passage. The grey area of adolescence is a scary place to be, especially if there is uncertainty about when it ends. The human spirit is capable of dealing with all kinds of stress, as long as there is a knowledge of an ultimate end to it. But the absence of a legitimate rite of passage leads to a serious breakdown in the process of a person's maturity. Children turn to all kinds of self-destructive activities in a futile search for adulthood. As they continue their search, what they are really wanting to know is, 'How many adult activities do I have to do before someone believes that I'm an adult?' Those activities or 'false rites of passage' include such things as using foul language, smoking, substance abuse, sexual encounters, pregnancy and (especially in the US) gang membership.

Foul language

This is usually where it begins, with the dirty words children learn in primary school (sometimes even as early as nursery school). Soon they realize that these are 'adult' words and their little minds quickly figure out that if they want to be a big shot with their peers, they should sprinkle in a few of these adult words. If I talk big, they assume, I'll be big.

Smoking

In a recent television interview I saw, nine- and ten-year-olds discussed the reasons why they began smoking. Almost all of them admitted that they lit up for the first time in an effort to look and feel older. Now these children are addicted to nicotine, but they still admit that they like the way they look when they smoke. Recent studies show that smoking among teenagers is on the increase.

Substance abuse

Drugs and alcohol are viewed as adult 'luxuries' by many teenagers so they use them as a rite of passage. The average age of first-time drug use among young people is thirteen, with some starting as early as nine. Warnings of the dangers of substance abuse and drug addiction are ignored by young people in their desperate attempt to find the activity that propels them into adulthood.

Sexual encounters

Having sex is viewed by many young people as the entrance into the world of adulthood. That first sexual experience is viewed as a rite of passage, until it actually happens. But instead of feeling like an adult, many young people tell of feeling let down, depressed and often suicidal. Jerry Johnston, in his book *Going All the Way*, says,

'Teenage years should be some of the most free, joyous years of life. For some, though, sexual experiences have created a tangled mess of emotions, leaving the kids bound in depression ... It is not uncommon for this disappointment to explode into a reckless "death wish." For innumerable kids, sex in the wrong way at the wrong time has been followed with a cloak of depression.'[2] Premarital sex doesn't cause teenagers to become adults, it only leaves scars that follow them into adulthood. However, it is important to realize that, among the many reasons teenagers give for engaging in sexual activity, wanting to 'feel like an adult' is an underlying factor.

Pregnancy

Although most teenage pregnancies are unplanned, many girls who do get pregnant choose to keep their babies and enter the world of childrearing. Becoming a parent, however, does not make them an adult. It is only after the baby is born that these young mothers realize this truth. Sometimes, boys believe that getting their girlfriends pregnant makes them a man. Willie, a teenager in Washington DC, broke up with his girlfriend after he found out she was using birth control pills. That changed their relationship, he said, because the girl would almost certainly not get pregnant. He commented, 'I couldn't feel like a man.'[3]

Gang membership

In places all over the US, young people are offered a rite of passage through gang memberships. To join the gangs, young people are often willing to endure a severe beating by members or participate in an illegal activity to prove toughness and value to the gang. They are initiated with the understanding that once in, they are no longer children, but adults. In most gangs, members engage in very dangerous adult activities, including drug dealing, armed robbery and murder. Young people who are desperate for a path out of childhood are easily enticed by these 'adult' activities that the gang provides. For some, life in the unpredictable and frightening world of gangs is a price they are eager to pay.

Gang membership is on the rise (and not only in the US). A study by the University of Southern California Center for Research and Crime found that street gangs operate in 94 per cent of all major cities in the US and can be found in at least 1,130 cities of all sizes. If a young person is looking for acceptance and a rite of passage, gangs are not hard to find.

These false rites of passage leave teenagers and young adults with a sense of emptiness. In addition to the dangers they pose, these activities can actually undermine the process of growing up by causing dependency. Successful rites of passage, however, allow children to step into adulthood in a healthy way that leaves them with the assurance that they are now considered adults.

What Makes an Adult?

A defined rite of passage helps a child to see him- or herself as someone who is prepared and expected to take on these responsibilities. In Jewish culture, the traditional celebration of the bar mitzvah symbolizes the passage of a thirteen-year-old male into adulthood. The celebration for females is called a bat mitzvah. Both events are still practised in today's society, but some argue that these ceremonies should be delayed because modern culture does not regard the age of twelve or thirteen as an entrance into adulthood. But twelve- and thirteen-year-olds are very capable of taking on some adult responsibilities, as we can see from the story of Jesus. Unfortunately in our modern times, they are rarely expected to take on these responsibilities.

The Rabbi Neil Kurshan, an enthusiastic proponent of modern-day bar/bat mitzvah, has this to say:

> I have often marvelled at the transformation which a bar or bat mitzvah can bring about in the life of a thirteen-year-old, who for the first

> time leads part of the service, shares in the religious honors reserved for adults, and speaks to all assembled about the significance of the occasion. Contrary to popular impression, the ceremony does not transform a thirteen-year-old into an adult overnight. After the [ceremony], a parent still lives with an adolescent who has to be reminded to clean up his or her room, to do his or her homework, and to help around the house. At its best, however, the bar mitzvah demonstrates both to the thirteen-year-old and to all those present that a young person is growing toward adulthood and toward responsibility and obligations to a broader community.[4]

As you can see from the Rabbi's statement, even in the Jewish culture the lines of adulthood are greyer than they once were. In the Israel of Jesus' youth, however, the line between childhood and adulthood was less ambiguous.

There are still some cultures that mark the passage from child to adult with symbolic ceremonies. In Mexico, fifteen-year-old girls are given a special ceremony called a Quincinera. Friends and relatives are invited to the festivity to help the girl celebrate her passage into womanhood. In parts of Africa and Australia, rites of passage for boys involve initiation ceremonies where they spend weeks or even months in a bush school or initiation lodge some distance from the village.[5]

Even in our 'western' society, less specific rites of passage have existed during various eras. When I finished high school at the age of eighteen in 1969, my graduation was a rite of passage for me. This was even more true for the generation preceding mine. American high school students were looked on as adults as soon as they received their diplomas, and adult responsibilities were to follow. Many of my male classmates found themselves in a strange, unknown country called Vietnam one year after graduation. Suddenly they were responsible for driving million-dollar tanks and defending their country. I don't think any of them gave much thought about whether or not they had passed into adulthood. The answer was obvious.

'The Waltons', a television show that was popular about twenty years ago, is about a close-knit family struggling through the Depression on their family farm. If you have ever watched an episode of this show, you have no doubt been left with the question, 'Whatever happened to the good old days?' I don't know a family that lives like the Waltons, do you? But, at that time in our society (1930–40), many families lived a rural lifestyle like the one depicted on that show. Several generations of a family often lived under the same roof, and the children were expected to begin the process of moving into adulthood as soon as they were old enough to take on responsibilities around the farm or house. As they grew older there was a progression in terms of the tasks they performed on the farm or within the household. By the time they left school, or sometimes earlier, they were equipped to go out and begin their own life. They had the advantage of knowing what was expected of them in a society and they had been given basic skills for living.

We have come a long way from the Waltons' lifestyle. We have great medical and technological advances that make our lives much easier, but we no longer give our children the needed transition from childhood to adulthood.

Leaving school is not necessarily a rite of passage today. Today, young people leave school and enter a world of confusion. They don't know what is expected of them. Much of society no longer believes it is their responsibility to define the necessary marks of passage from one social role to another. After many years of working with young people in the US, I have seen the fear they have as they receive their high school diploma and then try to answer the question from friends and relatives, 'What do you want to do with your life now?' They, and their counterparts in other western countries, are making a transition into the unknown and many of them are not prepared to meet the challenge.

When my buddies and I graduated from high school, we knew what we wanted to do, and we had been taught the skills to make it happen. We knew how to maintain a car, cook, and handle financial responsibility and all the things that kept us independent. We never dreamed of relying on our parents for the basic needs of life. Many school leavers now do not have the life skills to accept the responsibility of living on their own, even if it is just within a college hall of residence. We as parents need to provide opportunities for our children to step into adulthood.

When my sons were small, birthdays were a big deal to them, as they are to most children. Although some people might argue that this has more to do with getting presents than anything else, I disagree. Children like knowing that they are one year closer to being 'all grown-up'. And we know that teenagers long to be treated as adults.

A rite of passage sends a clear message to a child that it is time to begin to assume some of the responsibilities of adulthood. It helps them understand physical growth, mental development, identity and personality. A rite of passage also helps to define the parent–adolescent relationship – now they can relate to Mum and Dad as more of an adult than a child. Every parent should plan on discussing with their child the issue of a rite of passage. Parents and churches can work together to give children a defining moment when they know they have passed from childhood into adulthood.

When I was a youth minister, we provided several levels of mission work that were designed to help our young people discover that they were taking on an adult responsibility. For many of them, it truly was a rite of passage. First, our students were involved in working in a local homeless shelter for a week. We slept on the floor, ate in the soup kitchen, and got to know the people as they came to the shelter for help. The students were also given the opportunity to do mission work outside our own community in Laredo, Texas, where they worked with Hispanic migrant farm workers. Then before their final year at school, we offered the ultimate challenge: an overseas mission trip. In my present ministry at AWE Star, we have taken students as young as thirteen, fourteen and fifteen into third-world countries for thirty days at a time and watched as each one returned home a changed person.

I vividly recall Josh, a fourteen-year-old boy who had trouble communicating and taking on responsibility. He signed up to spend thirty days working in Budapest, Hungary, on an overseas mission trip. I challenged Josh, as I do all our students, that from this day forward he would be taking on adult responsibilities and adult tasks. He spent his time there working with the gypsy boys and girls. While there, he was responsible for making gospel presentations, working in summer camp facilities, and supporting the rest of his student team. I watched him transformed during that month, from a self-centred child to an adult who was focusing on the needs of others. When he returned home, his parents said he took on more responsibility in the home and that he actually began to look them in the eye when they talked to him! He was able to stand up in front of his church and speak about the wonders of God. His mother said, 'Our son was dramatically changed! He grew spiritually and mentally, and is now more responsible for his life.' I have never seen a teenager who has not been changed by a mission experience.

Many times, when these young people returned home from mission work after thirty days, their parents were able to provide them with a 'Christian bar mitzvah' where they shared their faith and testimony with their church congregation and received a blessing from their father who proclaimed that 'from this day forward, our child is an adult'.

As a parent you can plan ahead to send your children on an overseas mission trip as a rite of passage. Every child over thirteen is an excellent candidate for a global mission experience with an organization that provides both a rite of passage and adult tasks. Your church may be able to put you in touch with a suitable organization.

As parents, you have the choice: you can allow your children to continue their childhood even when their bodies are mature, or you can provide them with a rite of passage that will allow them to step into adulthood as fully mature people who are prepared for the journey that awaits them.

Thinking It Through

1. What rites of passage, if any, do you remember in your childhood?
2. At what age did your parents begin to give you some adult responsibilities? What were they?
3. At what age do you think adulthood begins in our society? Why?
4. Why is leaving school for the last time no longer a good enough rite of passage for young people?

Getting a Grip

1. Make birthday celebrations a big event in your home. Plan a special day with your child and emphasize the importance of being a year older. Make your child aware of some of the added responsibilities and benefits that will be coming his or her way in the coming year.
2. Give your child the experience of an overseas mission trip as a rite of passage. This is an excellent opportunity to show your child that you view him or her as capable of taking on adult responsibilities. View this as the line where your child crosses from childhood (adolescence) into adulthood and convey this clearly.

Chapter 2

Getting Satisfaction From Significance

Several years ago, I was lying flat on my back under our dilapidated old car doing minor repairs. I was tired and ready to get the job finished, when I noticed a little pair of legs standing by the wheel. My four-year-old son's little body appeared and I saw his blue eyes peering into the darkness under the car as he squatted down.

'Hi, Daddy,' he said, his eyes brightening when he saw me. 'Can I help you fix the car?'

In our hectic and fast-paced world, it's easy for us as parents to miss priceless opportunities with our young children, especially when we are busy. At unexpected times during each day, we can choose whether to make our children feel worthwhile and needed, or troublesome and incapable. With sweat dripping across my forehead into my ears and my hands covered with grease, I looked over at my son's little face and realized that this was a priceless opportunity. I could, in the next few moments, give him a sense of significance. The opportunity was in front of me and I had the choice whether or not to take it.

I smiled at my son and said with relief, 'Boy, Caleb, I sure am glad you came along. My tools keep getting away from me. Would you hold my screwdriver for me, son? That sure would help me get this job done faster.'

His eyes widened and he nodded so hard that his blond hair bobbed up and down on his head. I could almost hear him thinking, 'Wow, I came along at the right time! Dad can't get this job finished as quickly without me. I'd better hang on to this screwdriver because I've got a pretty big job here. I'm an important part of this family!' My wife, Cathy, came walking by and Caleb yelled, 'Look, Mom, I'm helping Dad fix the car!'

Caleb sat down beside the car and held that screwdriver tightly with both hands. For the rest of the afternoon he basked in the affirmation of those short moments helping his dad. He received a message that every child desperately needs to hear – that he was needed and capable.

Every Child Needs a Significant Task

Many children have never been given the chance to prove they are competent people. The adults in their lives miss many priceless opportunities to make them feel needed and wanted in their family by never giving them a significant task. A significant task is a task that will negatively affect other people if it is not carried out. Just as children need a rite of passage, they also need to feel significant. When we perform significant tasks, we begin to see ourselves as people who have purpose in life.

Let's go back to my favourite television family, the Waltons, for an example of family members with significant tasks. Seven children and four adults lived under one roof, so everyone had to do their share of the work or the household and the farm would fall to pieces. Suppose for a moment that young son Ben decides that he isn't going to cut the wood one day. That's his task and no one else is going to do it for him. Therefore, on that day when Ben doesn't cut the wood, no wood appears on the front porch. The grandmother, being the matriarch of the family, explains to Ben what will happen since he has chosen not to perform his significant task. There will be no wood for the stove, so there will be no breakfast, lunch or dinner, which means everyone in the family will be hungry all day. There will be no heat in the house, so the family will have to wear three layers of clothes or sit around all day huddled under blankets.

What if Mary Ellen chose not to perform her significant task, milking the cow? If she decides to sleep in on a cold January morning, instead of pulling on her snow boots and trudging down to the barn, there will be no milk for breakfast and no dairy products that day. The cow is soon going to become quite uncomfortable, and she'll dry up until she calves again. Do you see what happens? If Ben and Mary Ellen don't perform their tasks, other people suffer. That's pretty significant!

At the age of twelve, Jesus also had a significant task. He knew that it was the Father's will that He stay in Jerusalem after the Passover Feast and spend time in the temple with the rabbis. If He had gone against the will of His Father, He would have sinned and been unable to go to the Cross as the perfect sacrifice. His perfection hung in the balance that day. Salvation would have been lost for all mankind if Jesus had chosen to go back to Nazareth instead of doing His Father's will. I think being in the temple that day to assure salvation for the world was a pretty significant task for a twelve-year-old boy.

Jesus knew what His significant task was, and He took it seriously enough to put the will of His heavenly Father before the needs of His earthly parents. Children need significant tasks, and they need to know that those tasks are meaningful. If someone asked four-year-old Caleb what his significant task was on the day he helped me fix the car, his response would have been, 'I held the tools for Daddy so they wouldn't get away!' If someone asked Ben Walton about his significant task, he would say, 'I chop the wood so we can have heat for the stove.' Significant tasks give children the knowledge that they are needed and that they have a purpose in this world. Everyone wants that assurance.

When you ask adults what they do, they will answer with their significant task: 'I do accounting for an oil company.' 'I work with senior citizens in a nursing home.' 'I build houses.' 'I take care of my children.' Everyone wants others to know that they have a significant task. It gives them a sense of purpose in an otherwise purposeless world. When an adult loses their significant task, such as their job or the parenting role when their children go off to college, they often experience a sense of purposelessness and loss of self-esteem. Having a significant task to perform is one of the basic needs of all human beings. It validates who you are.

In my ministry, I work with teenagers from all over the country. When I ask them what their significant task is at home, most of them give me the same two answers: 'I make my bed and take out the trash.' I ask them a follow-up question, 'How many people will suffer if these tasks are left undone?' They think about it for a while and realize that no one will suffer if their bed is unmade or if the rubbish isn't put out for the dustmen. After I tell them the definition of a significant task, they stare at me blankly for a while. Suddenly, they realize the truth and they say, 'I don't have a significant task.' A teenager may have mastered the tasks of bed making and rubbish disposal years earlier, but they have not moved on to more significant tasks that take them out of the self-realm, and consequently they don't really feel that they are a significant contributing member of their family or society.

The Benefits of a Significant Task

Everyone wants to be needed. Even small children want to know that they are important to someone – usually Mummy and Daddy. As they grow, their desire to have a purpose and a meaning in this life grows as well. By the time they reach their teenage years, if the only significant task they perform is making a bed or taking out the rubbish, they will enter the real world searching for something that makes them feel needed. There are several things that a significant task does for a child:

1. It builds self-esteem

Caleb's task of holding the screwdriver made him feel capable, giving him the confidence to tackle a bigger job next time. As parents, it is our job to convey the message to our children that they are needed, wanted, and they matter in this world. They must first know that they are loved unconditionally by the God of the universe and that He sees them as a child of worth. This knowledge of God's love is foundational in preparing young people to enter a world that does not hold the view that each person is precious and unique. Children have a way of knowing who is 'in' and who is 'out', and if a child is already lacking in self-worth, their whole school experience can become even more painful if they are not part of the 'in' crowd. Children must know that they are God's special creation, unique and loved by Him.

We must then assure them of our unconditional love and tell them that we view them as worthy individuals. Unfortunately, actions speak louder than words and often as parents we undermine our words by our actions. If we are verbally telling our children that they are capable individuals, but never give them a task that allows them to prove that capability, then we have cheated them. We are not sending them the crucial message they need.

Educationalist Stephen Glenn writes in his book, *Raising Children for Success*, 'Children naturally want to help and to feel needed. They want to do *important* jobs. True, a small child cannot vacuum or scramble eggs as well as an adult, but with training they can do an adequate job. Besides, a job well done is not as important as helping a child develop skills and capabilities.'[1] As your children grow older they continue to build self-confidence as a result of the significant tasks they have been given. These significant tasks prepare them for bigger jobs that they will tackle with determination.

2. It makes them a functioning part of the family

Children born into families today are more likely to be considered liabilities than assets. In the US, for example, the estimated cost of raising a child through the high school years has climbed to $40,000. Add on college tuition and you're looking at over $100,000. That's a high-priced child! By contrast, in the days when children worked on the family farm, each child was considered an asset, worth about $5,000 of income annually.[2] In other words, that child was performing duties on the farm that would have cost $5,000 to hire out. So we have gone from viewing our children as functioning and valuable members of the family, to calculating how much they will cost us before they're out of the house for good!

Stephen Glenn writes, 'Research from many sources has made it clear that the stronger a child's perceptions of being an important, contributing part of a functioning set of relationships on an ongoing basis before the age of twelve, the more resistant he or she will be to peer groups, cults, and programming generally in their teens.'[3] How do you see your children – as liabilities, or as vital and needed members of your family? Your perceptions of your children are important. The way in which you view your children within your family affects how you treat them. If you see them as significant, you will give them tasks that prepare them to be capable people.

3. It makes them a functioning part of society

Psychologist and child-raising expert Kevin Leman says the training ground for life ought to be the home.[4] In our homes we should be giving our children the responsibilities that prepare them to step from the safety of the family environment into a world that is often unpredictable and harsh. If they have seen their role within the family as needed and meaningful, our children will probably find a place in our society where they can view themselves the same way.

The 'lost generation', or 'Generation X', is hungering to be a meaningful part of society. Generation X writer Janet Bernardi says,

'Since the fall of the Iron Curtain, some twenty thousand college-educated American twenty-somethings have moved to Prague to work as waiters, writers and English teachers. They are flocking to places where change is taking place rapidly and where their skills and energy can affect that change. There are many more examples of Xers heading in different directions in search of places where they might feel needed. It is their own search for meaning ... The people of my generation have been finding meaning in life by seeking out situations in which they may have an effect in the world.'[5] Significant tasks in the home give children a desire to continue to perform tasks within the world that make them an important part of a bigger picture. They begin to think of themselves as needed, not only within the family, but in the world.

Significant Tasks in the Home

Small children *can* do chores. This fact may be shocking for some parents. Let's imagine that your four-year-old comes bounding into the kitchen one evening and says, 'I want to help, can I wash the dishes?' Your first thought may be, 'I don't want to spend the rest of my evening picking up pieces of broken dishes and wiping water from the floor.' That's reasonable. So you tell your child, 'No, you run along and play, Mummy (or Daddy) will wash the dishes.' Now you don't have to worry about a mess. But be aware that when this same child, now aged twelve, is asked to come into the kitchen and wash the dishes, he probably will moan and groan and think it is highly unfair that he's being asked to help around the house. 'I'm just a child,' he thinks to himself, 'Mum and Dad are supposed to do the work around here.' And he slumps back down in the chair for a few more hours of television.

Allowing a four-year-old to wash dishes is risky. But most young children will gladly perform any task you give them as long as they perceive it to be one that is needed. The parents of the four-year-old could have agreed to let the child stand on a chair and rub the dishes with the soapy sponge while Mum and Dad stood ready to rinse and dry. This way, the child gets to help but the parents are nearby to make sure plates and dishes aren't broken.

Parents should begin to establish the principle of significant tasks early in the child's life. A very young child cannot be given truly adult tasks, but the parents should begin to build the perception of the child's importance and value to the family. In Caleb's mind, holding that screwdriver was a significant task. Now at eighteen, he would not see it that way, instead he would probably laugh and say, 'Get real, Dad, just stick it in your pocket.' Children should begin with small chores and escalate to larger ones as they grow up. Your diligence in making your children aware that they have an important role in the family extends beyond chores, however. They need to see themselves as people who help make family decisions and perform important family duties that affect everyone.

1. Family meetings

When my sons were growing up, we held family meetings every Friday night. This was an opportunity for Jeremiah and Caleb to have valuable input into the decisions that faced the four of us. Allowing them to express their ideas and opinions was crucial, but we also gave them a vote in important decisions. Be aware that when you give your children the chance to cast their ballot you might be outvoted! I can remember several family vacations that we spent in places that I had not voted on, but it was important for us to give our boys a chance to be part of the decision-making process.

When the boys were young the decisions they made did not have tremendous impact on our family (helping to plan the family menu or deciding what kind of dog food to buy). But as they grew older, the decisions carried more weight. We allowed them to be in on decisions such as what kind of car to buy and where we should buy a home.

When Caleb was fourteen and a high school freshman, he decided he wanted to change schools. He came to us and explained that the city had changed many of the school districts and now the friends that he had in junior high were going to a different high school. We told him that if he wanted to change schools he would need to find out what was involved in the process and be responsible for completing as much of the paperwork as he could. In several days he came home with the transfer papers, filled them out, and submitted them for school board approval. All I had to do was sign my name! The next term Caleb was attending a different school with his friends, not because of anything I had done, but because he had taken on the responsibility himself.

Major decisions like changing schools and buying cars were always discussed in family meetings. Sometimes the boys helped us make decisions, and sometimes they made decisions completely independently of us. My sons came to the family meetings with enthusiasm because they knew that their voices were always heard and their opinions counted. Young people and adults are much more motivated to follow plans in which they have ownership because of communication and collaboration. They feel significant and potent when they are involved in important decisions that affect them.[6]

2. Budgeting money

Discuss the family budget with your children and make them aware that you set aside a certain amount of money each month to pay utilities and other bills. One way to give your child a significant task is letting him or her write out the cheques for your household bills each month. You still have to sign the cheque, but the child is able to see how much money is going to pay for electricity, water, phone and other household necessities. This prospect may sound frightening, but it has many benefits. One of the hardest lessons to teach a child is the value of money. Sitting down and writing the amount on the cheque (twice!) reinforces that the things we take for granted cost money. It is also a quick way to show your child how expensive it is to run a household.

During your family meeting, you can reinforce the importance of paying the bills by educating everyone on what happens if the electricity bill is not paid (no lights), the water bill is late (extra fee), and the phone bill is forgotten (phone turned off). This last one usually hits home the most with teenagers. You might also have the child give a report on the status of last month's bill compared with the current month. Is the family using more electricity this month? Give the child the opportunity to lead the family in a discussion of what can be done to lower a particular utility bill next month.

One of the ways we taught our boys money management was to give them a clothing allowance. We contracted to give them a certain amount of money for clothes. For instance, we gave them $19 for jeans. We told them that they would be able to buy a good, durable pair of jeans for that amount of money, but probably not a pair with a fashionable label. If they wanted the label, they had to chip in their own money. It is amazing to watch how many times a young teenager will turn down a pair of trendy label jeans because they don't want to spend their birthday money on clothes! They were always having to make decisions on how to spend their money. The result was an increased awareness of the value of money – and the advantages of shopping in discount stores!

3. Reminding family of important responsibilities/appointments

An important part of running a household is car maintenance. When young, your child could be responsible for reminding Mum or Dad when the family car needs a service or oil change, and then when he or she gets a driving licence actually taking the car to the garage for maintenance. This is easier than it sounds, especially if your child is old enough to do maths well. Give your child a log book of how many miles can elapse between services, oil changes and tyre replacement. He or she can check the mileometer on the car and report when it's time for action. Be sure to include a time during the family meeting for the child to report on the car maintenance.

4. Community projects

Providing significant tasks outside the home proves to children that there are hurting and needy people out in the world. It is tempting to want to shelter our children from the unpleasantness of life, but serving others keeps us from building walls between ourselves and people in need. If your child has a heart for older people, make it a family priority once a month to visit a local nursing home. Find out what the needs are in your community and then talk to your child about what he or she would like to be involved in. Don't assume your child will want to visit sick people in the hospital if he is terrified of strangers. Learn what your child is gifted to do and find out what she has a heart for. Then find a place for them to serve where they are giving of themselves as they perform a significant task.

Five years ago I began a missions agency called AWE Star Ministries. The goal of the ministry is to help teenagers realize their importance and potential in the world by sending them on summer mission trips around the world. I tell them during our training sessions that from this day forward they are no longer children, but adults with a significant task to perform. They know that I expect them to take on the responsibilities of adults as we travel around Eastern Europe. It is amazing to watch as these young people meet the expectations that are laid out before them. When they know that someone else is depending on them, they see themselves in a new light, as a part of something bigger than themselves. A missions experience such as this will give your child a rite of passage and a significant task.

A Child Without a Significant Task

Today, there are hundreds of thousands of young people who really believe they have no purpose in the world. They may choose to give up and 'check out of life', or they may begin to search for a place where they can find meaning and purpose. These children will do anything to feel they are part of something important. Gangs give young people the illusion that they have crossed over into adulthood and offer them false significant tasks to perform. The gang membership offers them a significant task of protecting their 'turf' and each other. They are even willing to die for each other. Those tasks are taken seriously by these young people because they have never had a role to play anywhere else, including in their family.

How many of you parents find yourselves constantly in the car driving your children from place to place, and from event to event? Every day there are vanloads of parents criss-crossing every town or city with their children. Why? Because your children, without a significant task at home, look for other ways to fill that need. Some do it with sports teams, others with music lessons. Your child *will* find a significant task somewhere.

I am a baby boomer. I was born on a farm, but my parents moved to the city when I was two. I am a part of the first generation that did not have a significant task built into my home life. Because we all need a significant task, I found something to do. I started the '60s! Well, not all by myself. There was a whole group of us out there needing the same thing. Many of us in America filled that need by protesting against the Vietnam war and 'teaching' the rest of the world how to live in harmony. Do you know what ended the '60s? We got jobs, had children and found ourselves with *real* significant tasks.

We are the first generation to attempt to raise and educate a whole generation of young people who do not have a significant role to play in the culture. Each year we bring well over 3.5 million children into the world who are not needed or even expected to be significant in the economic life of their family.

These young people are also born into a culture that no longer offers the stability of rituals, traditions and activities that validate and reinforce their role in the culture.

From the cradle to the twentieth year of life, many children in the West are told, 'Keep your mouth shut. Stay out of difficulty. Get good grades. Do what we tell you.' They are not told, 'You are absolutely critical to the survival of our family. We need you. We could not accomplish what we do without what you have to offer.'

A primary reason for the decline in motivation, discipline and achievement in schools is the incredible passivity involved.[7]

What if I hadn't recognized the opportunity to give Caleb a sense of significance the day I was working on the car? Assume I was already in a bad mood and that I viewed Caleb's offer as an intrusion. I could have sighed loudly and said to him, 'Caleb, go on into the house and play. Daddy's tired and he needs to finish this job quickly, I don't need you in the way right now.'

I can picture what Caleb's face might have looked like at that moment. The smile would disappear quickly and as he slowly turned to go, he might be saying to himself, 'I guess I'm not big enough to do anything to help Daddy. All I can do is play. Gee, he must think I'm not very important around here.' At the age of four, his thoughts probably would not have been that crystal clear, but children have an amazing way of picking up the messages we send them. Children need self-esteem, and to know that they matter in the world. You can tell your child this, but you must also give him or her the opportunities to prove it.

Rising to the Challenge

A few years ago, I was with a group of young people on a mission trip to Eastern Europe. While there, we were invited to a prison camp in Szeged, Hungary, which had been run by the Communist Party a few years earlier. We were the first group ever to visit the prisoners and share the message of Jesus Christ. The prison was hidden far back in the woods and it was surrounded by high fences topped with circles of barbed wire. We were escorted into the prison and got our first look at the prisoners. They were led through a door and they immediately rushed to the front row when they saw girls in our group. They were sullen men with tattoos on their arms and mismatched uniforms.

Our drama team shared the message of the gospel in the tiny, sweltering room with sweat pouring down their faces. When the crucifixion scene began, the sound of the nails being driven into the hands of Christ bounced off the concrete walls and we began to see the sullen expressions change. All of a sudden the prisoners were leaning forward, focused on the boy who was portraying Christ.

When the drama ended, the warden stood up. He told the men that we would be available in the prison courtyard for anyone who would like to talk or ask questions about the message they had heard. The prisoners were led out of one door and we were led out of another. We had not planned to answer questions after the performance; we assumed that we might talk to one or two prisoners and be on our way. It had been hard to read their faces, and we wondered if they had understood any of the message. We entered the small courtyard and before us stood every prisoner, eagerly waiting to talk to us. They were packed together, watching us with questioning eyes. Quickly our young people organized the prisoners into lines and for two hours, these thirteen- and fourteen-year-old boys and girls patiently listened, answered questions, and prayed with the prisoners through an interpreter.

Some of the men rejected Christ, but many were saved that day. I'll never forget how one giant prisoner hoisted one of our young men on to his shoulders and walked through the crowd pointing at the boy and saying, 'He told me about Jesus, he led me to Jesus.'

Before we left, the warden climbed on to our bus to say good-bye and to thank us for sharing with the men. 'This place,' he said, 'will never be the same after today.' As we were riding back on the bus, I asked the young people how they were feeling about what had just happened. One girl spoke up immediately, 'What if we hadn't come here today and shared with them about Jesus? They might never have heard and then they would be lost forever!'

God used those teenagers in a mighty way that day, and they realized the significance of it. They saw the challenge that was ahead of them and they had the confidence in themselves to tackle it.

We as parents have a challenge ahead of us also. We must take the time to give our children the significant tasks they need. I stress the word *time* because you can't do it on the run. Conducting family meetings, teaching your children to pay the bills, helping them be involved in community projects, and developing other avenues to significant tasks involve commitment from parents. When we take the time to give our children a sense of purpose in life, we are helping to develop capable young people into capable adults. Today's children, who are tomorrow's adults, will suffer if they go through life without a rite of passage and significant tasks. Unless we diligently seek to provide both of these for them, we will all pay the consequences.

Thinking It Through

1. If, as a teenager, someone had asked you what your significant task was, what would you have answered?
2. Examine your perceptions of your child. Do you see him or her as significant in the family? What tasks do you give your child to make him or her feel significant?
3. How do you communicate to your child that he or she is precious and unique?
4. What significant tasks send the message to a three- to six-year-old that they are a vital part of the family? What significant tasks can you give your children?

Getting a Grip

1. Evaluate whether the tasks your children are performing are taking them out of the 'self-realm'. Do they meet the definition of a 'significant task'?
2. Make a task chart for your children and list what each child does. It helps for a child to see this in writing and know that the family is depending on him or her to carry it out.

3. Schedule a night for family meetings and let the children help decide the agenda for what is to be discussed. Let each child have a turn contributing during the meeting, whether it is voicing an opinion, helping develop a solution to a family problem, or reporting on a task he or she has performed that affects the family (such as paying the utility bills or scheduling car maintenance).
4. Sit down with your child and talk about projects in the community that he or she might be interested in. Find out what they have a heart for and what their gifts and talents are so you can help guide them into a community project.

Part II

Conflicting Moral Standards

Getting a Grip on Teaching Values

Chapter 3

Shopping in the Supermarket of Values

The plane was still filling with people as I sat down wearily in my seat. It had been a long weekend and I was about to shut my eyes when I saw him. His hair was long and stringy and his face was nearly hidden by a long beard and thick moustache. He wore a Hell's Angel leather vest and tattoos covered his arms and chest. A long, gold chain hung around his neck and several earrings dangled from each earlobe.

People were shifting in their seats, probably hoping his seat wouldn't be next to theirs, and as he passed by my row I glanced at what he was carrying. Suddenly, I sat up straight. In his arms, the biker carried a doll that was dressed in a matching leather vest and a gold chain around its neck. A gold hoop earring dangled from the doll's soft round nose and over each of its plastic eyes the biker had placed a skull-and-crossbones sticker. This was a stuffed doll with attitude! The biker carried it loosely in one arm, as if he was afraid he might injure it if he squeezed the doll too tightly. He looked as if he was carrying a child.

I closed my eyes and leaned my head back on the seat, pondering what I had just seen. It seemed to me that here two value systems had come together. The biker represented the generation that has grown up knowing all about drugs, alcohol, sex and rebellion. They are the 'me first' generation. The doll represented all that is innocent and good – sharing, honesty, purity, others first and all the 'traditional' values taught to previous generations. It was a true picture of the two opposing value systems that exist side-by-side within the young people of this generation.

Our society seems more confused than ever about values, and parents are groping for ways to pass on their own values to their children. All around us, we see our culture continually challenging our beliefs.

A few years ago, I was called into the principal's office at my son's school. It was Caleb's first day of kindergarten, and I when I entered the office, I felt my stomach lurch. This was a place I had tried desperately to avoid during my school years, and now I had received 'the call' about my child. I sat down in the wooden chair, my palms sweaty and my mouth dry.

What, I wondered, could Caleb have done that was so terrible on the very first day of kindergarten? I pictured a food fight in the canteen or maybe a skirmish in the playground. But on most days, Caleb was a well-behaved child so neither of those things seemed likely. The principal entered and I stood up quickly and shook his hand. He smiled and motioned for me to sit back down.

'What happened?' I blurted out. I was never good at small talk.

The principal continued to smile for a moment, then became serious as he relayed this story:

The first day of kindergarten had begun smoothly with the teacher writing her name on the blackboard and proceeding to talk to the children about what was expected in her classroom. After a few minutes Caleb's hand was up.

'Yes?' she said, stopping in mid-sentence.

'Do you know Jesus Christ as your personal Lord and Saviour?' he asked loudly.

The teacher was unnerved and she replied, 'Put your hand down, please. We don't talk about that in class.'

There was silence for a moment, then she continued addressing the class. She had barely resumed talking when Caleb's hand shot up once again.

'What is it?' she asked Caleb, this time a bit annoyed.

'You know, if you don't, you're going to hell.'

And now here I was in the principal's office, not because my son was involved in a food fight or a playground skirmish, but because he was repeating what he had heard all his life. The principal leaned forward across his desk and said to me, 'I appreciate Caleb's concern for his teacher, but that is not our value system here. We don't discuss those things in the classroom.'

I told him I understood and promised him I would talk to Caleb about it. But even as I said it, I knew it would be difficult to explain to my five-year-old about different value systems. From the time he was born, he had lived in a home where we talked openly about the need for a relationship with Jesus Christ; now he was entering a world where that subject was not an acceptable topic for discussion. We had tried to raise him in a home where Christ was honoured and followed, where Scripture was learned and practised, and where God was the ultimate authority. We had talked openly of these things. Now within the walls of his school, he was not going to be able to talk openly about spiritual things without the danger of being reprimanded or ridiculed.

Suddenly the value system Caleb was being taught was going to be challenged from all directions.

Where Have All the Values Gone?

Chuck Colson, who was an aide to President Nixon during the Watergate scandal, and who is now a believer and head of an international prison ministry, noted a few years ago that our culture is not teaching the *wrong* values as much as it is teaching *no* values.[1]

Values are crucial in a society and in a family. Without moral standards as a foundation, people are doomed to drift endlessly through life, searching for truth but never finding it. Our values are the yardstick by which we measure our attitudes and behaviour. Increasingly, however, our society is losing its yardstick and there seems to be nothing consistent against which we can measure ourselves.

My own country, the US, for example, has always been a mix of many different cultures. The people who settled here brought with them distinct values and traditions as they banded together in communities across the nation. The value systems within those communities were basically unchallenged and they shaped how each member of the community viewed the world.

I grew up in a neighbourhood where the lines between right and wrong were very clear. My family, neighbours, teachers and peers had the same value system. Everyone who surrounded me in my childhood world, including role models from TV or the movies, supported the same value system as my parents.

Now in our neighbourhood, my son's world is bombarded with mixed messages about what is right and wrong. His peers are grappling with choices between good and bad, and society's selection of role models is frightening. Today's youth don't see many adults who live by absolute values. They see people such as some evangelists who are supposed to live a moral and upright life, but fall into immoral behaviour, and presidents who are caught in compromising situations. So instead of finding good role models, young people are often forced to settle for heroes whose personal goal is making money, not developing and exhibiting character. Parents who are trying to raise responsible young people with a solid value system are worried that perhaps they are fighting a losing battle.

Where Are We Shopping for Our Values?

When I look around at society, I am struck with the same feeling I get when I am shopping for a soft drink. It used to be easy to make choices. When I was a child, my friends and I rode our bikes down to the corner shop for a fizzy drink almost every day after our chores. When we peered into the big white bin that held the cold drinks, we were faced with the same three choices – Coke, Dr Pepper or a grape

Nehi. It wasn't a tough decision. I always chose the grape Nehi.

Now when I go to the shop to choose a soft drink I have many decisions to make. First, do I want one with sugar or a sugar substitute? Do I want it with caffeine or without? Do I want it cherry-flavoured and fizzy? A lemon and lime flavour and still? A cola with sugar but without caffeine, or maybe without sugar and with caffeine? Suddenly my head is spinning and I'm more confused than ever. And I get thirstier, so I reach for the same old thing every time.

For the first time in history, our children no longer have just one or two value systems to choose from. For them, society is like a supermarket, with rows and rows of values to choose from. As our society has become more mobile, we have taken our cultural and family value systems and moved to places where the values may be different. No longer are our children living in a society where they are surrounded by people with similar value systems, instead they receive hundreds of conflicting messages every day about right and wrong. As parents, our voices must be heard loud and clear above all others, but it is becoming increasingly difficult to drown out the negative messages.

Johnny is a child who lives in a town called Anywhere. He attends Anyschool and is a typical twelve-year-old boy who loves to hang out at Anypark and rollerblade down his street, Anylane. Let's follow Johnny through a typical day to find out what kinds of messages Johnny is receiving that might affect his value system.

1. Peer group

Johnny takes the bus to school and is offered a seat next to Bobby who is also twelve. Bobby loves to use newly acquired adult words and to tell jokes he has heard his dad tell at weekends after playing golf. Bobby tries to talk Johnny into joining him and a few other boys after school at the park to look at some magazines he had found under his dad's mattress last weekend. Johnny hesitates. 'Oh, come on,' Bobby says with a smirk. 'A whole bunch of us are coming along. You'll miss out if you're not there.' Johnny promises to think about it.

2. Music

During the lunch hour Johnny notices some of the boys listening to headphones and he asks what music is playing. Ricky pulls out a case of CDS and tells Johnny to pick out something he wants to hear. Johnny peeks into the case and sees quite an array of popular music. The CDS contain songs such as 'Help Me, I am in Hell', 'The Art of Self-Destruction', 'Scum', 'We Don't Exist', 'Dried Up, Tied and Dead to the World', 'Misery Machine' and 'Irresponsible Hate Anthem'. Johnny closes his eyes and picks one.

3. Television

After his homework is done, Johnny decides to relax so he grabs the remote control and plops on to the couch with a bag of crisps and a Coke. Although there is a commercial on one channel, Johnny watches it anyway because it is one of his favourites. It shows two men on the beach surrounded by a group of bikini-clad girls who are pulling beer out of a cooler one by one. The music is upbeat and it has a funny ending that always makes Johnny laugh. He flips through the channels and passes a rerun of a steamy, late-night soap opera, a film where he hears a stream of expletives, and a pop music programme where he watches the group whose music he heard on the CD at school.

4. Media

Johnny has a homework assignment that includes clipping articles out of the newspaper. So Johnny takes some time to read some of the events of the day, which include a murder in Anytown, a child abandoned in Anypark and a violent robbery on Anyblock. He doesn't find what he needs in the paper, so he flips through his sister's fashion magazine where he sees articles such as 'Getting What You Deserve in Bed', 'Women Who Have Been Date-Raped' and 'Climbing the Corporate Ladder Faster Than Your Friends'. Johnny also sees advertisements for cigarettes, beer, diet plans and sex manuals. Not finding exactly what he thinks will please his teacher, he logs on to the Internet. Before long, he has 'stumbled' on to a real-time chat room, where his female counterpart is offering him something much more exciting than a homework assignment.

These are only a few of the messages that Johnny receives in a typical day. From the time he leaves home in the morning, until the time he goes to bed at night, Johnny has been exposed to very few God-honouring values. Chances are, you live with a Johnny in Anytown.

Why Do Children Need Values?

Children need boundaries. It is a well-kept secret that children even like boundaries. They need the security of knowing there are values that the family lives by, despite the messages that the world is sending. If we don't communicate our values to our children then we have sent them out on a violent sea without a compass. They will be tossed back and forth by the wind and have no sense of direction. Former US Secretary of Education, William Bennett, says this in his insightful book, *The De-Valuing of America: The Fight for Our Culture and Our Children*:

> What determines a young person's behavior in academic, sexual and social life are his deeply held convictions and beliefs. They determine behavior far more than race, class, economic background or ethnicity ... If that soul is not filled with noble sentiments, with virtue, if we do not attend to the 'better angels of our nature', it will be filled by something else ... As the Roman scholar Pliny the Elder put it, 'What we do to our children, they will do to society.'[2]

I can hardly imagine a society that has lost all its values, but our society seems to be drifting in that direction. As parents, we must talk to our children about our faith, and what that faith means to us.

How to Bring Back the Values

Faith in God

Moses wanted the children of Israel to remember their faith when they entered the Promised Land. God gave Moses the wisdom to know that once the people had tasted prosperity, it would be easy to forget all that they had been taught. Their minds would be so filled with their new home and the 'good life', that the blessings God had given them could be easily shoved into the dark corners of their minds. So he told them:

> These commandments that I give you today are to be upon your hearts. Impress them on your children. Talk about them when you sit at home and when you walk along the road, when you lie down and when you get up. Tie them as symbols on your hands and bind them on your foreheads. Write them on the doorframes of your houses and on your gates.
>
> (Deuteronomy 6:6–9 NIV)

We can spend time with our children talking about our faith as we walk, in the evening before bed, in the morning before they go out to face the world, and every other opportunity that comes our way. Very young children are already impressed and awed by God's creation. We can take advantage of that by talking about the love God shows for us in the way He has put our universe together. Spend an evening with your child under the stars, lying on the ground looking up at the vast expanse of the sky. Conversations about God's greatness and glory will flow naturally as you look up, and you can use this opportunity to talk about why it is important to obey and follow God, the Creator of the universe.

One evening when we were finishing our family devotion with prayer, six-year-old Caleb suddenly stretched his neck and bent his head downwards, attempting to lay his cheek flat over his heart. He looked like he was in pain, but he began to pray aloud. His voice sounded as if he had just inhaled a helium-filled balloon because of the crimping of his airway. It was so funny to see him pray in this contorted position that we couldn't help laughing out loud.

'Why are you praying like that, Caleb?' we asked him.

'I'm praying like our pastor,' he replied.

I had been praying with our pastor and watching him pray for many years, but had never seen him twist his body like that during his prayers. He is a very distinguished man.

The next Sunday during the worship service, Caleb nudged me in the arm during prayer time. 'Look, look,' he whispered, pointing to our pastor. Sure enough, he had his head bent down to the middle of his chest and was speaking into the microphone clipped to his tie. Caleb was unaware of the fact that every week during the offertory prayer, the pastor talked and prayed with our radio audience.

'See,' Caleb whispered proudly, 'Jesus lives in his heart and he is talking to Jesus right now, before he preaches, to make sure he has the right sermon.'

Caleb had been watching the grown-ups around him and had learned from them that we can pray any time and anywhere. We must impress upon our children the importance of having values that honour God, values that they can hang on to when life's storms get rough. Children are longing for a foundation that is strong and that will hold up even when everything else around them seems to be crumbling.

Countering negative messages

If we are going to communicate values to our children, we have to be prepared to talk to them about the messages that are contrary to our value system. For instance, if they go to a friend's house and watch a television show that they are not allowed to watch at home, how will you respond? If you only lecture them about how wrong it is, you have done more damage than good. Sit down with your child and talk about the show. Ask them to describe what values they thought were being taught in the show, then talk about whether those are your family's values. Be prepared to answer questions from your child and use the opportunity to communicate why you want to pass along values that honour God.

As children get older, they will make decisions every day about values. Many of these are decisions that we as parents cannot control. We can only instil and communicate our values early on, and continue to pray for our children as they choose a value system for themselves.

Modelling values

I began thinking seriously about this issue of values when one of my sons came home from school and repeated the adult words he had heard from his friends and I was shocked. And that was kindergarten! I decided I should determine how to communicate godly values to my children. I went to the Scriptures and found a passage that struck me as simple, yet profound. 'Jesus began to do and to teach' (Acts 1:1 NIV).

Jesus knew that despite all the hours He had spent with His disciples talking to them and teaching them about the kingdom of God, they would understand it best if He lived it out in front of them. That's why on the night before His arrest, He chose to spend part of the evening bending over them washing their dirty feet, instead of talking to them about servanthood.

> So he got up from the meal, took off his outer clothing, and wrapped a towel around his waist. After that, he poured water into a basin and began to wash his disciples' feet, drying them with the towel that was wrapped around him.
>
> (John 13:4–5 NIV)

Only after He had shown them what to do, did He tell them how to do it and the value of it.

> Now that I, your Lord and Teacher, have washed your feet, you also should wash one another's feet. I have set you an example that you should do as I have done for you.
>
> (John 13:14–15 NIV)

Jesus was a role model for every value He wanted to teach His disciples. I realized that I had to live out the values that I was teaching my children. I can't count the number of times I have pointed to my sons and asked my wife in frustration, 'Why are they acting like that?'

When Caleb started playing basketball he loved the crowd's response as much as the game itself. Every time he would get the ball, instead of hurrying to the basket with it, he would head for the sideline where he would dribble the ball down the court as close to the onlookers as possible, grinning like a Cheshire cat at the crowd all the while.

The first time I saw him do this, I turned to Cathy and said, 'Where in the world does he get that?' She smiled calmly, turned to me and said, 'Have you ever noticed that every time you shoot the ball and it goes in, you look at the crowd and grin?' Without even realizing it, I had role-modelled for my son that you were supposed to please the crowd when you play basketball. Children learn more from seeing than from hearing.

I have worked with many teenagers whose parents want them to attend church but don't attend themselves. They want so much for the church to teach their children values, that they will go out of their way to drop them off and pick them up at numerous church events and camps. Sadly, I have also watched these same young people drop out of church several years later and proceed to get into all kinds of trouble. They had been watching the values of their parents very closely and ultimately adopted that value system. Confused parents have come to me and said, 'I don't understand why they're in all this trouble. I sent them down to "that church" to learn some values, and now look at them!'

What parents fail to realize is that their children have been watching them more closely than anyone or anything else. I have learned that I must be role-modelling in my home everything I want them to learn. We cannot teach one value system and then live another. Our children's eyes are upon us all the time. They are going to watch what we do to see if it matches up with what we say. If we

live out what we believe day after day, then they will know that we are serious about our values.

Thinking It Through

1. What value system are you passing on to your child? What do you spend your time doing that reflects your values?
2. What do you do to share your faith with your children throughout the day in various ways?
3. How do you counter the negative messages that are passed on to your child throughout the day? Are you able to talk openly with your child about why those negative messages are not a part of the family value system?
4. What do you need to change to better model the value system you want your children to have?

Getting a Grip

1. Write down on paper what you consider to be your family's value system. Sit down with your family and talk about why these values are important to you.
2. Consider having a family devotion time each morning or evening, and encourage honest and open discussion during this time. Be aware of opportunities during the day to talk about your faith with your children.
3. When you have to make a choice in your life about values, sit down and talk with your children about the choice you made. For instance: 'Today my boss asked me to do something in my job that I felt was going against something the Bible tells us to do. I want to tell you about the decision I had to make today …'
4. If your child brings home music or a video that you believe goes against the value system you are trying to teach, take the time to listen to the music with your child or watch the video with them, then discuss it. Ask them what values they see being promoted in the music/video.

Chapter 4

Living With Logical Consequences

Morning mist still hung on the leaves of the tree and she could smell the fragrance of its fruit as she stepped closer. She noticed how the tiny drops of water on each piece of fruit sparkled in the morning sun, making each of them almost untouchable and too perfect to disturb. But her mouth was watering.

She had been eyeing the tree for a while now, watching the fruit grow and change colour: white, green, pink and now red. She had tried often to imagine what it might taste like and had spent afternoons sitting beneath the trunk of a nearby tree watching the leaves flutter in the soft warm wind. Now she was so close to the tree that she could smell the fruit and touch the lowest branches. She lifted her hand and with one finger stroked a leaf, then pulled her hand down quickly to her side. Her heart was pounding, and the words He had spoken were still fresh in her mind, 'For when you eat of it you will surely die.' She shuddered.

But the serpent had seemed so wise during their conversation earlier that day. 'Of course you won't die,' he had said in a warm and friendly voice. 'God wouldn't do that, He just doesn't want you to know that when you eat the fruit, you will become like Him! You'll know everything, won't it be wonderful?'

She stood at the base of the tree, wringing her hands and glancing behind her. Adam was watching her with a frown. I don't want to die, she thought, but the serpent must be right. God wouldn't do that. I'll just take a little bite and see what happens.

She stood for a few seconds longer, glanced at Adam one more time, then reached up for the fruit. She started to pick a large apple, but instead chose a smaller one. 'Just a tiny one,' she whispered. 'What's the worst that can happen?' She plucked it from the branch, smiled at her husband and took a big bite.

Learning the Art of Choosing

When Adam and Eve ate from the tree of the knowledge of good and evil, God did not have to shout and stamp and say, 'How many times have I told you? I've told you over and over and over again, leave that tree alone! If I've told you once, I've told you a thousand times, don't eat from that tree!'

No, God simply said, 'You eat, you die.' It was that simple. Those were the logical consequences of tasting the fruit, and Adam and Eve both knew it. Logical consequences are the expected results of an action that we have chosen.

God doesn't want children who are preprogrammed to love and obey Him, He wants us to choose that for ourselves. God wanted Adam and Eve to choose whom they would follow. He knew that eventually other voices would invade the garden and that upon hearing them His children would have a choice to make. You and I are like Adam and Eve. Every day, a thousand voices push their way into our homes, our schools, our offices, and we must choose whether to listen and follow. These are the choices God allows us because He doesn't want robots, He wants personal relationships.

Likewise, as parents we cannot choose for our children whose voice they will follow. Children can be guided towards the right values, but they cannot be forced to choose those values. We can do everything possible to model and talk about our values around our children, but they must own those values for themselves by choosing them. How do we teach children to choose right values?

Like anything else, they learn by practising. We give them opportunities to practise making choices. They will experience the logical consequences of these choices, both good and bad, and they will begin to understand that good choices bring pleasant consequences, bad choices produce painful consequences.

It isn't easy to allow children to choose. It's so much easier for us as parents to choose for them. We reason that because we've been down the roads of life and learned so many painful lessons along the way, we can save our children all that heartache by telling them which roads to avoid. And we tell them what they should believe and how they should behave. But I'll tell you a secret – they'll sit quietly and listen to us and nod understandingly, but then they'll head down those same roads unless they are given the tools to learn how to choose for themselves what values to embrace.

So how do you help your children learn to choose? I'll give you some examples from our experience. Read these, but decide what is best for your family and get creative! You are your child's first and most important teacher, so come up with a plan and stick with it.

Good Word, Bad Word

Filthy language coming from the mouth of a five-year-old is enough to make any parent go through the roof.

When my oldest son, Jeremiah, was in kindergarten, he came home from school one day clutching his little lunchbox and smiling proudly. Grandma was visiting and he bounced into the living room and stood in front of her where he proceeded to let out the most shocking 'adult word' you can imagine. It was one of those words that sort of hangs in the air above you after it's been spoken.

'Where did you hear that word?' I bellowed as I towered over my little boy. I could see Grandma's mouth hanging open as she prepared to cast out demons. Jeremiah looked up innocently and replied, 'School.' I looked into his eyes and said, 'Do you know what it means?' I could have guessed his reply. 'No,' he said softly, looking curiously at my red face and the veins standing out on the side of my forehead.

I realized I had to do something to help my son get a grip on the many conflicting value systems that surrounded him. This was the beginning of the Good Word/Bad Word project. That evening, I took a large piece of paper and made two columns, one for good words, one for bad words. I told Jeremiah that we would develop a chart and after our evening devotion we would discuss words he was unsure about and decide where to place them, either in the 'good word' or 'bad word' column. One stipulation: he could not repeat the word that he had heard during the day until it was on the chart. After he told me what the word was, I explained its meaning and let him decide which column to place it in. If he decided it was a bad word, we chose two good words to replace it and wrote them in the good word column. Each evening, as we filled in our chart, he began to assign value to words. With our guidance, he chose what value to place on each word.

In three years we had every swear word in the English language posted on the chart. Eventually we had no more words to add to the bad word column. It's amazing the communication barriers that go down when you are writing down filthy words with your children. We also, however, wrote words that carried confusing meanings. We were able to talk about subjects like homosexuality and abortion before our children reached nine years of age! Opening up this kind of communication gave my children the knowledge that their parents would not over-react or be shocked at anything they wanted to discuss.

Once the Good Word/Bad Word project was under way, my reaction to the 'adult words' that the boys brought home was controlled and I realized that talking about these words opened up other avenues of discussion. Without this project, my boys would have endured years of seeing Dad seethe with anger over words they heard at school, and the only lesson they would have learned would have been, Don't say the bad words in front of Dad. Instead, at a very early age, they learned that there are things that are good and things that are bad, and they must develop the skills to know the difference. Learning these skills helped them to assign value to other parts of their lives. Throughout their lives Jeremiah and Caleb will continue to make choices, but I believe learning to make those value judgements at an early age prepared them for the bigger choices they have had to make along the way.

When he was a freshman in high school, Jeremiah came to me and told me he had made the choice not to drink or have premarital sex. He realized that this was a choice that he had to make, his mother and I could not make it for him. So at the age of fourteen he chose a certain value system.

Four years later, when it was time to choose a date for his senior prom, he was again faced with a choice. He did not date much at high school, but he wanted to go to the prom so he had an important decision to make. For months he agonized over who to ask. It was a choice that he was making on his own. Finally he made a choice, he asked her to the prom, and she accepted.

The night of the prom arrived and Jeremiah picked up his date and brought her back home to introduce us. When they walked into the room, my knees grew weak. She was very tall and very, I mean very, mature looking. When I was in high school we never had any girls who looked like that. He introduced her to us and told us that she was a freshman. A freshman? My son is taking a freshman to his senior prom? Very concerned, I motioned him to join me in the kitchen and as we walked I thought to myself, I wished we lived in the 'old days'. Cathy and I should have been busy these past few months matchmaking. We could have chosen from dozens of girls we knew and Jeremiah would have had the distinction of being the only senior at the prom with an 'arranged date'. Besides, didn't parents do that in the Bible? I sat down weakly in a nearby chair like an old man.

'Jeremiah,' I said, 'what were you thinking, son? A freshman?' I discreetly counted on my fingers, 'that's a three-year difference, you know.'

'Dad,' he said, 'I looked through all the school, and I chose this girl for a reason.' I raised my eyebrows. 'What reason?'

'Because she was the only girl in our school who had the qualities most like Mom.'

There was a silence and I felt I would choke on my words so I stood and led him by the arm into the living room. I looked at the very mature-looking girl in her fancy prom dress and smiled a fatherly smile. 'Go and have yourselves a good time,' I said, thinking what a wonderful girl he had found.

Jeremiah had once again made a choice based on a value system that was his own.

Teaching Values Through Logical Consequences

Adam and Eve knew the consequences of their sin. As the perfect parent, God made His children aware of the consequences they would suffer if they disobeyed Him. Children like to know the rules before they play a game. They don't always follow the rules, especially if they are losing, but they like to know the rules just the same. And in our homes, children want to know what is expected of them, they want boundaries. But get ready, once you set the boundaries in place, they'll test them many times to make sure those boundaries are firm.

We taught our children logical consequences by contracting with them. Just as God made a contract with Adam and Eve, we made a contract with our children so they knew the boundaries and the consequences if they crossed those boundaries. The Bible is a contract. The old contract, the Old Testament, is a contract between God, 'Yahweh', and His chosen people, the children of Israel. The new contract is outlined in the New Testament, quite simply, the Gospel of Jesus Christ. This new contract is very simple, accept Jesus Christ and you receive eternal life. So contracting is not a new idea, in fact, it began in the garden. God made a verbal contract with Adam and Eve: I'll allow you to live, if you don't disobey Me by eating from the tree of the knowledge of good and evil. It was fair and it was clear.

We are a generation of parents, however, that has done everything in our power to make sure our children are kept far away from logical consequences. If our children make a mess of things, we fix it for them. See if the following scenario sounds familiar.

It's bedtime for the family and suddenly little Susie says, 'Oh no! I forgot I have a science project due tomorrow!' Susie is in tears and her parents look at each other in horror. Suddenly Mum and Dad spring into action. They make a late-night run to the supermarket to get supplies and stay up half the night constructing a volcano that spews out red jelly when a button is pushed. Of course everyone knows who put together that little project ... Mum and Dad! The only thing Susie learns from this is that there are no serious consequences for putting off important homework assignments because Mum and Dad will be there to bail her out.

We are raising a generation of children who are skipping down the road of life assured that Mum and Dad follow two steps behind, cleaning up their clutter. Granted, children will mess up. It's a part of growing up, and we need to give them the assurance that our love is not based on their perfection. But we must also love them enough to let them fall, feel the pain and get back up again. Life is like that. We go through life learning, hurting and growing. Susie would have learned a valuable lesson, and one that she probably would not repeat in the future, if Mum and Dad had simply let her deal with the consequences on her own. 'It's your science project, Susie,' Dad could have said. 'You're going to have to come up with something in the next eight hours on your own. Mum and I have to go to bed.' It sounds harsh, but learning lessons the hard way is what makes it a lesson.

Wanting our own sons to learn as painlessly as possible that their actions have logical consequences, we sat down with them and explained that we would like to put some of our expectations in writing. We made a contract with our sons.

The first one was very basic with just a few sentences. We signed it, then they signed it and each of them kept a copy of it in their rooms. Once a year we renegotiated the contract and made sure that their responsibilities grew each year. Included in the contract was everything from pet care to care of their clothes and property. Here are several examples of our contract:

Valuable and valueless

Every material possession falls under one of these two categories. In our house, we determined what was valueless just by looking on the floor. Finding a path to the bed, chest of drawers or wardrobe in my sons' rooms was like scouting out trails on a hiking expedition. We jumped over pieces of Lego, waded through piles of shoes and stepped carefully over mounds of clothes. Cathy, the family laundry expert, became particularly enraged by the mounds of clothes, so we decided to take action. We put an agreement in our contract that if certain items of clothing spend a significant amount of time on the floor, we will deem them valueless. And, we told them, guess what we do with things that are valueless? There is a wonderful place in our town that turns these valueless items into valuable items – the charity shop. So we have contracted with our boys that anything on the floor that shouldn't be there is taken to the charity shop.

When I tell this to parents, they shake their heads in despair and say, 'My children would be naked if I did that!' And I tell them, 'That's the logical consequence! But they wouldn't be for very long.' You see, once a few favourite pieces of clothing are hauled away, they begin to catch on to the idea of logical consequences, and hangers and drawers look much more appealing.

Transportation to and from school

We told our boys that we would be responsible for getting them to and from school, which meant we paid fifteen dollars a month for school bus transportation. If they decided to mess around with friends after school and weren't where they were supposed to be, they missed their bus and had to find another way home.

When Jeremiah was twelve he approached me after dinner one night and told me he had to talk about something that happened at school. 'What's happened?' I asked. He paused for a moment and said, 'Well, see, I was sharpening this pencil at school today, and I was flipping it with my fingers and all of a sudden it stuck in the ceiling. And then the teacher walked in and ... well, I have detention tomorrow.' I nodded with parental understanding. 'That's no problem,' I said. He looked relieved. 'So you can come pick me up after detention?' I looked at him sadly, 'I'm afraid not, son.' He looked shocked and I continued, 'You see, we have this contract, remember? It says that I pay a certain amount of money for you to take the school bus to and from school. I've taken care of my part of the contract so I'm afraid you're on your own.' He looked at me with sad eyes, 'What am I gonna do?'

'I don't know, Jeremiah, what are you going to do?' He sat down and thought. I threw out some ideas. 'Maybe you can ride home with your teacher, she's the one who gave you detention. Or how about the janitor? I've seen lots of movies where the janitor is the last one to go home; he'll probably still be there, won't he? Or you could just walk home. It's only three miles across two major freeways. Or you could take a cab.' By this time Jeremiah was looking panicked and I put my hands on his shoulders. 'Son, this is your responsibility, you're on your own.'

So Jeremiah went to school the next morning and I watched him go, firm in my resolve to let him experience the consequences. His mother was not so sure. The minute he stepped out of the door Cathy began to worry and fret. 'I'm taking the car and following him home after school,' she said. I told her I had full confidence in our son that he would find a way home. So I came home early from work to make sure she didn't have to worry and fret alone. We stood and watched his bus come and go, then we stood for another hour, her fretting, me worrying.

At four-thirty I heard something pulling into our driveway. Looking out of the window, I saw Jeremiah getting out of a Yellow Cab. Slowly, unzipping his little cowboy wallet, he began to hand money to the cab driver. Jeremiah walked into the house, sullen. 'How was school today, Jeremiah?' I asked cheerily. He marched through the living room and said, 'Five dollars and ten cents.' I smiled. At the age of twelve, Jeremiah knew the price of detention: five dollars and ten cents. And several years later when his younger brother, Caleb, came home with a sad story of detention the next day, he already knew the consequences. So he asked if he could pay me the $5.10 to pick him up at school. I accepted his offer.

Both of my sons learned from these experiences that they were responsible for their actions, not just at home, but at school also. Many children think that the world will clean up after their mess just like Mum and Dad do at home. They learn a hard lesson later in life. When I was a youth pastor, a parent called me to ask if I would get her son out of jail. When I asked what he had been arrested for, she said, 'He robbed a late-night store, that's all.' I told her I would not bail him out because at this very moment he was learning a valuable lesson about logical consequences. Chances are, this young man never learned these lessons at home, and now he was paying the price in a big way.

Providing clothes

One part of our contract with the boys is that we will spend $50 each winter for a new coat. We take them shopping, tell them they have a limit of $50, and let them pick any coat they want at that price.

When Jeremiah was twelve years old, he lost his brand-new coat at a football game. He came home and told me this and I promptly replied that I was sorry to hear about his misfortunes. He wanted to know when I could buy him another; I reminded him that I had already taken care of my part of the deal. 'I bought you a winter coat, Jeremiah,' I said. Once again, he asked me the familiar question, 'But Dad, what am I gonna do?' I shrugged and he stomped off to his room. A few minutes later he returned and held up his piggy bank, 'I've got three dollars.' I shook my head, 'Where do you think you're going to find a coat for that amount of money?' He thought for a moment and said, 'You know that place where we take all our valueless stuff to make it valuable? You think they might have something?'

So Jeremiah and I drove to the charity shop to look for a winter coat. We entered the shop and trudged around for quite a while before we found one with a price tag of three dollars. It wasn't a pretty coat, though. It was old and it had been torn and patched in several places. But he dumped the money out of his piggy bank and bought that sad, old coat.

The next Sunday we walked into church as a family: Cathy in her elegant long wool coat, me in my classy black overcoat, and Caleb in his sporty leather coat. And with us, Jeremiah, trying to hold his head high, wearing a three-dollar patched coat. It was a humbling moment for him. But he hung on to that coat for the rest of the winter and now he says it was the best coat he ever owned. Why? Because it had value. He paid for it with his money and he knew that if he lost it, Mum and Dad were not buying another one.

Getting to school on time

When I preach in other cities I often stay in people's homes and I am convinced that when it is time for school, families across the country are living out this same scenario:

Mum and Dad wake nine-year-old Johnny up and immediately say, 'Now we have to hurry and get ready, go and eat your breakfast.' Johnny rolls out of bed and plods to the kitchen where he stares at a bowl of cereal. Meanwhile Mum and Dad are passing in and out of the room with gentle reminders, 'Hurry now Johnny, eat that cereal and go and brush your teeth.' He chokes down the cereal and strolls leisurely back to the bedroom where the toy he was playing with last night catches his attention.

Mum and Dad are now in the doorway with nervous faces, 'Go and brush your teeth, come on, hurry, hurry. We're going to be late.' Johnny lumbers into the bathroom, brushes his teeth at a pace that makes Mum and Dad even more nervous, heads back into his room and stares at his wardrobe.

By this time, his parents are pointing furiously at the wardrobe and snapping their fingers. 'Get those clothes on. Hurry, Johnny,' they chant together as he slowly begins to pull his clothes on. Dad is pointing at his watch and Mum continues the chant, 'We're going to be late, hurry, we're going to be late, quick, we're going to be late ...' He finally gets his clothes on but stares around the room blankly, 'Where are my shoes?' Mum and Dad both groan loudly and tear through the house looking for the shoes. Johnny shrugs, looks under his bed, and finds them. Mum and Dad are now shouting and following Johnny to the door like coaches cheering on their athlete in a race, 'Come on, get that bag, find that coat, let's go, we're late already, get a move on, you can do it!'

Each morning Mum and Dad leave the house in a fury, lecturing Johnny all the way to school about the virtues of learning to get ready and out of the door in a timely fashion. But Johnny isn't listening. He knows that Mum and Dad will be there again tomorrow morning, reminding, chanting, yelling and following him to the door for the final cheer. It's not a bad morning routine for Johnny. He doesn't have much at stake.

But what would happen if tomorrow morning Johnny's parents decide to take a different approach and put Johnny in charge? How, you ask, can they possibly do that?

In the morning they wake Johnny up and say, 'At 8.00 a.m. we will leave for school. You will get into the car at that time wearing whatever you have on. If you only have your underwear on, you still get in the car. If you are not wearing your school clothes, in the back seat of the car there is a sack which contains an entire set of clothes. These clothes do not match, they are wrinkled and they smell a little funny. But that is what you will wear to school today if you choose not to get ready by the appointed time.'

Johnny will probably think about it for a minute or two, decide they're bluffing, and carry on with his usual slowcoach routine. But after a few days of wearing the 'sack clothes' to school, Johnny will no longer need any help getting ready for school. He will hop out of bed each morning and get himself ready in a flash, because he has learned that the logical consequence of not being ready on time is ... the SACK! Oh no, not the SACK!

Negotiating Logical Consequences

Children learn the art of negotiation early in life. They start arguing and bargaining before you've had time to learn to defend yourself. It is natural. They also learn early in life that it feels good to have input into family decisions. This is also natural. So you can combine these two natural desires and give your children a significant task – they can help negotiate their contract!

For instance, let's say you sit down with your child and let her negotiate the consequences for going down the street to play without telling you. You might say, 'I think you should be grounded for a week.' She says, 'I'd rather you just take away spinach for a week.' Knowing she hates spinach, you reply, 'No, we must agree on a consequence that disciplines you for your actions.' So you ask her what she really enjoys. 'Television,' she replies. 'I suppose you could take away television. But only for two days?' And so you go back and forth with your child until you have reached an agreement. Now she has had input into what will happen to her if she does something wrong. She is clear about the consequences because she has helped decide what they will be.

When Caleb was given detention at school, he already knew there would be consequences, but because of his brother's experience he also had the skills to negotiate in the situation. He knew we were open to this and he came up with his own logical consequence for his actions. He paid me to pick him up.

When children help decide the logical consequence of their actions they become much more responsible for those actions. They are no longer left to wonder if they can 'wriggle out of this mess'. They begin to take ownership for the choices they make each day. Susie knows that if she makes the choice to go down the street without telling Mum or Dad, she will live with the consequences she has helped negotiate. The choice becomes fully hers: go down the street and play without telling Mum or Dad, or enjoy the privilege of television. She can't have both.

Choosing a Value System and Understanding the Consequences

As children grow older, the choices they face will become increasingly more complicated. Choosing the right value system can be a matter of life and death. As parents we must guide our children towards a value system that glorifies God, but we cannot make their choices for them. We can, however, give them opportunities in the home to practise those choosing skills. And that requires that we open up communication with our children. I practised this with my boys using the Good Word/Bad Word project. It gave us the opportunity to talk openly about many subjects that were uncomfortable, yet they were able to choose for themselves the value of the words.

They also learned through logical consequences that they are responsible for the actions they choose. If our children do not learn this they may drift from one value system to another, or allow someone else to choose their value system for them. They must be prepared to experience logical consequences in life. And when they help to negotiate their contract, they know that they have taken part in deciding their own logical consequences.

It is never too late to begin. You will have to decide, based on your child's age and maturity, what to include in the contract, but here are a few ideas: Clothes must be in the laundry basket or they will not be washed and the child will have to wear smelly, wrinkled clothes. Younger children need to make their beds before school or they will lose the privilege to play outside with friends or watch television. Older children must abide by their curfew or they will suffer the consequences of not going out with friends.

Your children should help decide the logical consequences. As you talk with your children about what they think the consequences should be, you are helping to develop good communication skills with them. When the consequences have to be put into place, there is no screaming, lecturing, or arguing because you and your child have both had a part in deciding ahead of time what the discipline will be.

As parents, we need to pray for wisdom in how to help our children learn to make choices and deal with the consequences of those choices. God has entrusted us with our children, they are gifts from Him and we must seek to develop them for His kingdom.

Thinking It Through

1. What choices do you allow your children to make during the day? Do you find it easier to make their choices for them?
2. Think back on yesterday. What values did you communicate to your children? Did you spend time with them? Did you talk positively about other people in front of them? What things do you wish you had done differently?
3. Are there times when you try to force values on your children? How do they respond?
4. What tools are you using to help your children choose godly values?

Getting a Grip

1. Find creative ways to help your children learn to choose values. Consider the Good Word/Bad Word chart or another method that helps them learn to make choices.
2. Begin to practise logical consequences. Contract with your children and give them a voice in negotiating those consequences. Post your contract in a visible location and make sure both you and your children sign it.
3. Watch television with them, read magazines together and listen to their music. Ask them what values are being advocated in each of these.

Part III

Help, My Baby Has a Beard!

Getting a Grip On
Today's Escalating Sexuality

Chapter 5

PMS in the Playground

Dear Mum and Dad,

I know you are disappointed in me and I wish there was some way I could make you happy again. I wish I could go back to the way things were when I was a little girl ... before I started having all these feelings inside. It seems like one day I was a normal kid, ignoring all the boys at school and playing with my friends, and the next thing I knew all the boys and girls were getting together and doing grown-up things.

I try to control my thoughts but I keep having fantasies about sex. My body keeps growing and changing and I don't know what to do with it. I wanted to talk to you about it, but I was ashamed and confused. And now I know that you are going to be embarrassed to be seen with me. I just wish someone had told me that all of these feelings I have inside are so dangerous.

I miss seeing you smile at me. I am sorry that I had sex with Tom. I am sorry that I got pregnant. I know that things will never be the same again for me or for you. I was so excited about starting at that new school next month, now I feel as if my life is over.

Please forgive me.

Your little girl,
Amy

Amy is twelve years old. She hit puberty two years ago and has been dealing with a variety of emotions ever since. At the age of twelve her ability to make rational decisions is limited, yet her body is now capable of much more than she realizes. She is surrounded by images of sex and her friends have been talking more and more about losing their virginity. For Amy, making the right choice about sex was even more difficult because she felt she could talk to no one, including her parents. They were confused by her sudden growth spurt and they seemed almost ashamed that she looked more like a woman than a young girl. There are millions of children like Amy, dealing with the onset of puberty at a very young age, yet not knowing how to handle the accompanying emotions.

In Josh McDowell's book, *What I Wish My Parents Knew About My Sexuality*, one teenager writes:

> ... we [teenagers] are still developing and we're in a very precarious period in our lives. During these years our minds are developing as well as our bodies and we seem to be 'stuck' in between childhood and adulthood. We, more than adults, desire to be accepted by our peers. We desire friends and are beginning to be attracted to the opposite sex during this time. Our sexual feelings are very strong, and there have been times when I feel like a 'hormone with feet'. You might laugh at that but I'm serious when I say that a teen's emerging sexual desires are very strong, and without a fully mature mind to control that teen, peer pressure can be a very loud voice.[1]

Like Amy, many young people are confused and frightened by these strange new feelings that accompany puberty. And parents are also frightened. We are watching our children, sometimes as young as eight years old, begin puberty, and we are afraid to talk to them about sex. The thought of sitting down with a child that young and talking about conception may terrify us, but now more than ever we must help our children get a grip on their own sexuality.

The Mind of an Adult, the Body of a Child

Emily was ready. The dress had been cleaned and pressed, her wedding trunk had been full for almost two years, and her future husband was putting the finishing touches to the tiny house they would move into after the wedding.

She and her mother had made sure all of the things she would need for her new life were already in the house: a new stove, butter churn, washboard, sewing kit. The honeymoon would consist of one night and one day in their new house without any chores. After that, real life would begin. They would wake up and her husband would walk to the barn to start his day. Emily's day would start in the kitchen. In addition to the usual cooking and washing, her day would probably include gathering eggs, churning butter, planting corn, mending clothes and feeding some of the animals.

The only thing Emily was unsure about was her first night with her husband. Although her mother had told her everything she needed to know, Emily was still afraid she would not be ready. Sex was not something she had thought much about. In fact, she was not even sure her body was ready for it. But, she was in love and ready to make a life and a family with her future husband and she was certain that whatever happened in the bedroom they could learn about together.

There were so many responsibilities ahead of her, but at the age of sixteen, Emily was ready.

Sweet Sixteen and Setting Up House

Emily may have been your grandmother. In the early to mid-1900s, a young woman preparing for marriage was ready to run a household and in rural areas to help her husband run the farm. She had all the skills to handle life. From a very young age, her own mother had been teaching her the skills she would need. She was ready to take on these adult responsibilities. She had a significant task. It was not unusual a hundred years ago for a sixteen-year-old woman and an eighteen-year-old man to be entering into marriage with the blessing of their families. In times past, marriages generally tended to be made at younger ages. Two hundred years ago, for example, under common law in the United States, a woman could marry at twelve and a man at fourteen. Today in the US and many other countries the legal age is eighteen for both men and women.[2]

Even though Emily was emotionally prepared for marriage, physically she was not as mature. At sixteen she had just hit puberty. The hormones raging around in her body were new and she was just getting used to the monthly cycle that had started last year.

> Before 1850 the average woman first menstruated at about sixteen years of age. Dr Grace Wyshak and Dr Rose Frisch at the Harvard Medical School and the Harvard Center for Population Studies reviewed more than 200 studies including more than 200,000 women between 1795 and 1981. ('Evidence for a Secular Trend in Age of Menarche,' *The New England Journal of Medicine*, 29 April 1982, pp. 1033–1035.) Not a single one of the sixty-five studies done before 1880 found an average age below fourteen and a half. Many were seventeen or more. By 1950 however, the average was down to about twelve and a half or thirteen.[3]

When Bach was choirmaster at St Thomas Church in Leipzig, more than two hundred years ago, boys often sang soprano until they were seventeen. Tenors and basses were men whose voices had already changed. Altos were those whose voices were changing. In 1744, Bach had ten altos, the youngest was fifteen and the oldest nineteen. Men's voices changed at about seventeen years of age then, but now this happens at about thirteen or fourteen (J.M. Tanner, *A History of the Study of Human Growth*, Cambridge University Press).[4]

Most couples who married in the early part of the century learned about sex from their spouse. Since there was not a large gap of time between puberty and marriage, and because sex before marriage was not socially acceptable, young people did not have the enormous sexual temptations that adolescents face today.

A Child's Mind Trapped in an Adult Body

Andrew hit puberty before his parents were prepared. At twelve he began to grow hair under his arms and parts of his body began changing and enlarging. Although he still acted like a child, his parents were aware that he was looking more like a man. Andrew's father thought about sitting down with him to discuss all the physical changes and what those changes meant, but he rationalized that because his son still acted like a little child, he wouldn't understand all of it. I'll wait until he's older, he thought as he watched him wrestle on the floor with his younger brother. Sex, he concluded, doesn't mean anything yet to him anyway.

Lori's parents faced the same thing as Andrew's parents. At the age of ten, Lori was the first girl in her class to buy a bra. Soon after that she began shaving her legs, and the next year, aged eleven, she started her periods. Lori's mother watched her daughter's development helplessly, and wondered if she should begin talking to her about sex. She decided against it. She's still a child, her mother thought, sex is something she won't deal with until much later.

Recently I was speaking to a group of adults, many of whom are primary school teachers. After our session we talked about what is going on in schools today. They began telling me about eight- and nine-year-old girls in their schools who were hitting puberty.

The reality of this is that young girls who are still learning basic spelling and maths are faced with the menstrual cycle. As they are playing hide-and-seek in the playground, they are dealing with raging hormones. I can picture the fight over a swing between a young pubescent girl and a confused classmate. PMS in the playground.

Dr Ronald Kotesky in his book, *Understanding Adolescence*, says, 'Today we think of puberty as the time when people are first able to have children. The dictionary tells us that, but it also tells us that the word *puberty* comes from a Latin word meaning "adult". That is, among the Romans and throughout history, *puberty* was the beginning of adulthood itself, not the beginning of a stage between childhood and adulthood.'[5]

As we discussed in Chapter 1, we no longer allow our children to jump straight from childhood to adulthood; instead, we offer them an extended stage prior to adulthood called adolescence. During this stage, young people have the physical characteristics of adults, but still behave like children. I am constantly amazed at the appearance of the young men and women I work with in my ministry. Many of the teenage schoolboys have full beards, something I never saw twenty years ago. Growing facial hair when I was at school was considered a feat. In my high school, the only person with a full beard was ... the principal!

Today, however, teenagers look older. The hormones kick in sooner, causing the young person to experience sexual desires for the first time. American statistics suggest that every ten years children are reaching puberty six months younger.[6] Twelve-year-old girls have the hormones of a twenty-year-old flowing through their bodies and they don't know what to do with them. If parents are uncomfortable talking to their children during this stage of life, the potential for disaster is present. An ignorant adolescent with sexual desires is a walking time bomb.

Our children are living in a confusing world that glorifies sex and discourages virginity. Our children are dealing with adult hormones at younger ages, but still think and act like children. All of these factors make it difficult for us as parents to relate to what our children are going through, but it is more vital now than ever that we seek to understand the pressures that surround them.

Dealing With the Desires

We live in a changing world. Children are moving into puberty at earlier ages and they are faced with desires that lead them into adult activities and adult consequences, often before they get a driving licence! The average age of marriage today is twenty-four for females, and the average age of puberty is twelve. So there are millions of children out there who are dealing with unsatisfied raging hormones for at least twelve years. Many of them choose to satisfy their desires without waiting for marriage. For many adolescents, dealing with the desires means giving in to them. With so many pressures internally and externally, many young people decide that sex is just not worth the wait.

People magazine had a cover story titled 'A Shocking Poll of Parents and Kids: What You Don't Know About Teen Sex – How Often They Do It and How Little They Tell'. Even a secular magazine is shocked about the sexual experiences of our young people!

Our children are surrounded by sex. Peer pressure, sexual images on television and in music and pornography all contribute to how often our children give in to the sexual desires within them. What can we do as parents to help them get a grip on those desires?

Sex Education in the Home

I remember the first time my son asked me about homosexuality. He was six years old. It's a scary moment to realize that your child is wanting to delve into a subject that you can't explain in one sentence. I would like to have smiled at him and said, 'Now you run along and don't worry about grown-up things like that.' But I knew better. I was aware that at his young age he wouldn't be able to comprehend a detailed explanation, so I gave him as much as he could handle. I told him that God's plan was for a man and a woman to marry, and that God said for a man to marry a man was wrong. I left it at that, but he knew that the door was open to bring this subject up again. We had established open communication, and over the years we were able to talk openly about all aspects of sex.

As parents we are responsible for preparing our children to enter the world. We want them to be able to make wise choices, but they cannot do this without information. Sex education in the home is vital as our children are experiencing sexual desires early in life. To be able to choose for themselves what their values will be concerning sex, they need:

Accurate information

Talking to a child about oral sex, conception, menstrual cycles, sexually transmitted diseases and orgasms will strike terror in the heart of even the most stalwart parent. Suddenly your palms are sweating, your face is red, and you are stuttering through each sentence. But if the thought of sex education in the home frightens you, consider this: sex education on the bus. Or sex education in the changing room. Or sex education in the bedroom of a classmate. Parents, if your children can't get the information from you, they'll get it somewhere else. And chances are, the information they receive out in the world won't live up to your value system. We'll talk more in the next chapter about how to talk to your children about sex.

God's view of sex

Sex is God's idea. And He must think it's a pretty good one, because He is very clear about how precious and sacred sex is between a married man and woman. In fact, He devoted an entire book of the Bible to sex. Tucked between the books of Ecclesiastes and Isaiah is a steamy poem written by King Solomon. If you think sex is something that God is shy about, consider these verses:

> How beautiful you are and how pleasing, O love, with your delights! Your stature is like that of the palm, and your breasts like clusters of fruit. I said, 'I will climb the palm tree; I will take hold of its fruit.' May your breasts be like the clusters of the vine, the fragrance of your breath like apples, and your mouth like the best wine.
>
> (Song of Songs 7:6–9 NIV)

Because sex was created by God, we can teach our children that He has a purpose for it. It is holy and is to be kept within the confines of marriage. God knew that if we took sex out of the marriage bed, we would experience emotional, mental, spiritual and physical pain.

After twenty-five years of working with teenagers, I could fill a book with stories of students who are living with the pain of guilt, low self-esteem, unwanted pregnancy, sexually transmitted diseases, and AIDS. When we break God's laws, they break us. He desires to protect us from these hurts.

Standards

Our children must know where we stand on the issue of sex outside marriage. The world does not set a standard; instead, it says if you love someone, sex is the natural way to show that love. But we must hold to the standard God has set before us, and communicate that to our children. 'It is God's will that you should be sanctified: that you should avoid sexual immorality; that each of you should learn to control his own body in a way that is holy and honourable' (1 Thessalonians 4:3–4 NIV).

Communication

We must let our children know that they can come to us with any question or any confession. Many children fail to receive timely counsel because of parental denial, gullibility, or indifference. As a result, children often make poor sexual choices. We just don't want to believe our little Mary or Bobby does those things. To avoid the pain of confrontation and reality, we choose to hide our heads in the sand.[7]

Our children need someone they can trust as they enter into the turbulence of puberty. Their minds are still developing and they need continual guidance and understanding. We cannot simply hope that they will pick up our values concerning sex. As parents, we must make a firm commitment to open the lines of communication and help them choose their own sexual values.

Thinking It Through

1. What questions do your children ask that might open the lines of communication about sex? Do you take advantage of these opportunities?
2. How comfortable do you think your child is about his or her body?
3. Are you prepared for your child to begin puberty at an early age? Will you be willing to sit down and talk with him or her about the physical and emotional changes that are occurring?
4. What factors do you think have caused puberty ages to drop in the past two centuries?

Getting a Grip

1. Ask your adolescent to sit down and tell you how he or she feels about the physical changes he or she is experiencing. Offer to answer any questions about those changes.
2. When your child comes home repeating 'adult' words that deal with sex, take the opportunity to explain what the words mean. Even very young children can be taught that sex is holy and reserved for a married man and woman.
3. Talk to your children about sex in the media. Sit down with them and watch a television show, then discuss it. Ask what sexual values, if any, were being promoted.
4. Hug and kiss your spouse in front of your children and talk about the feelings of love you have for one another. Children need to see many examples of healthy relationships between a husband and wife.

Chapter 6

The Battle for Sexual Purity

Mike was struggling. Like most adolescent boys, he was often distracted by sexual fantasies and found it difficult to ignore the myriad of sexual images that surrounded him. As a Christian young man, he wanted with all his heart to stay pure until he married, but his body and the world around him were trying to convince him to give in.

Mike shared his struggle with me one Sunday night after church. He approached me in the hallway and stood for a few moments looking at his feet. 'I need to talk to you about something that's going on with me,' he said quietly and I waited for him to continue. The words finally came. 'I'm having these bad thoughts ... sexual thoughts. Every time I look at a girl I start thinking about ...' His voice faded and his pimply cheeks turned a deep red, 'I'm afraid I'm a really bad person.'

I assured Mike that he was a healthy, normal male adolescent. Hormones are a part of life, I told him and he smiled. But I quickly got serious and told him how dangerous hormones can be if standards are not in place. 'You are going to have to put all your heart and soul into resisting temptation if you want to stay pure,' I said. Mike nodded. 'I want that . . . to be pure,' he replied.

Over the years Mike continued to struggle with temptation. Pressures from friends constantly forced him to defend his decision.

Sexual films, music, commercials, television shows, magazines, calendars, posters and advertising hoardings surrounded him. And the hormones flowing through his body continually beckoned him to give in to his desires.

Mike married a girl from our church quite a few years later. The morning after their wedding the phone rang at my house. I answered it. 'Hello, Brother Walker, guess what? It was worth the wait!'

It took me a few moments to shake myself out of a sleep state before I realized who was calling. 'Mike?' I asked. 'Is that you?'

'It's me, Brother Walker.'

'Mike, you're on your honeymoon!'

'Yeah, Brother Walker, I know. And I just wanted you to know that it was worth the wait ... you know.'

Mike's story has a happy ending for both him and his wife. This couple was able to come together for the first time and share the most intimate expression of love. Their wedding night was not filled with pangs of guilt or haunted with memories of previous partners. They shared a gift that each had reserved for the other and in doing so, fulfilled God's plan for their marriage.

I wish each married couple could share the joy that Mike and his wife experienced on their wedding night. Unfortunately, the statistics tell us that most adolescents begin having intercourse in their mid-to-late teens, about eight years before they marry.[1] It's obvious that there are thousands of couples out there beginning married life already having experienced what God designed only for marriage. One young husband described his relationship with his new wife this way: 'I had several physical relationships with girlfriends before I married. Now, whenever I kiss my wife or engage in love play, I think back to the other women. One girl could kiss better than my wife, another girl was better at something else and so forth. I can't concentrate on loving my wife with my total being – there have been too many women in my life to be wholly committed to one.'[2] As parents we need to begin talking to our children about 'how far is too far?' We cannot withhold the information they need to make the right decision about their sexual purity. One quick talk about the 'birds and the bees' or a stack of books from the library will not suffice. We must be there to help them get a grip on learning the value of sexual purity and the dangers of premarital sex. But first we must be sure we understand these values and dangers ourselves.

Sex in the Garden?

God knew that there was no creature on earth that could satisfy Adam's longing for a mate, so He created one. Only God knew exactly what Adam needed, but instead of creating this 'helper' from the dust of the earth as He had done with Adam, God chose to make her from the man's flesh and bone. Both Adam and Eve were created as sexual human beings. Until they gave in to sin, they were a perfect model of God's plan for a husband and wife. Their relationship included complete, innocent and open oneness, without a hint of shame.[3]

After creating Eve, God gave the couple instructions: 'Be fruitful and increase in number' (Genesis 1:28 NIV). God told Adam and Eve to have sex. It was His idea first! He created both the male and female bodies with sex in mind.

Many of us think of sex as something that God is ashamed of, but 'God saw all that he had made, and it was very good' (Genesis 1:31 NIV). God created not only sex, but sexual desires. God designed us to be turned on by the opposite sex, but he designed those desires for only one person, our spouse. When the Bible says, 'a man shall leave ... and cleave' (Matthew 19:5), it means that the couple will be permanently glued, or cemented to one another.

The Bible is very clear about the purpose of sex. It is not to be cheapened by making it a recreational sport that we participate in with a variety of willing partners. Sex is holy because it was created by God, and the Bible is very clear about how we should use this holy gift. It is for procreation, pleasure and an expression of love between a husband and wife.

Moses told us, 'For this reason a man will leave his father and mother and be united to his wife, and they will become one flesh'

(Genesis 2:24 NIV). Jesus said, 'Haven't you read ... that at the beginning the Creator "made them male and female", and said, "For this reason a man will leave his father and mother and be united to his wife, and the two will become one flesh"? So they are no longer two, but one. Therefore what God has joined together, let man not separate' (Matthew 19:4–6 NIV). And Paul wrote this in a letter to the church of Corinth, 'Do you not know that he who unites himself with a prostitute is one with her in body? For it is said, "The two will become one flesh" '(1 Corinthians 6:16 NIV).

All of these verses point to one truth: sex bonds two people together in a private, personal, and spiritual way. Our teenagers need to understand that every time they engage in sexual intercourse with someone, they are leaving a part of themselves behind with that person. Teenagers need to know that having sex unites them to a person emotionally as well as physically. Physical relationships are easy to discard, but emotional ones are more difficult. Even the acts that lead up to intercourse are a part of having sex, and our teenagers must be aware of this before they begin going out with a girl- or boyfriend.

Sex Is a Progression

Her name was Debbie and she was the prettiest girl in church. I was in seventh grade, aged 12, and without a girlfriend so I decided to pray about it. 'Please, God,' I pleaded, 'give me a girlfriend. I *need* a girlfriend.' God is merciful, and Debbie finally gave in and told me she would 'go with me'.

So there we were, sitting together in a Sunday night church service. Since my prayers had been answered and Debbie was now officially my girlfriend, I decided the time was right to show the world that she belonged to me. So I did the old 'yawn trick', raising my arms dramatically above my head during an exaggerated and hideous yawn, then lowering one arm carefully around her shoulder innocently. She pretended not to see, but my heart started beating so fast I thought I might faint. I looked around to see if anyone else could hear it pounding, but no one seemed to notice. Everyone around was completely oblivious to my plot. I, however, could hardly sit still.

It was a sexual feeling to have my arm around Debbie's shoulder. But after a few weeks of cuddling, the sexual feeling it brought was no longer a big thrill and I decided it was time for something a little more serious, like a kiss. Once my most primal desire had been satisfied, I had to move to the next level. Sexual desires are like many others: the more you have, the more you want. I didn't get any further than a little peck of a kiss, but I learned an important lesson from my first girlfriend. Those first sexual feelings are great, but they wear off.

Sex is not one final act, it is a whole series of acts that lead to intercourse. The scale looks like this:

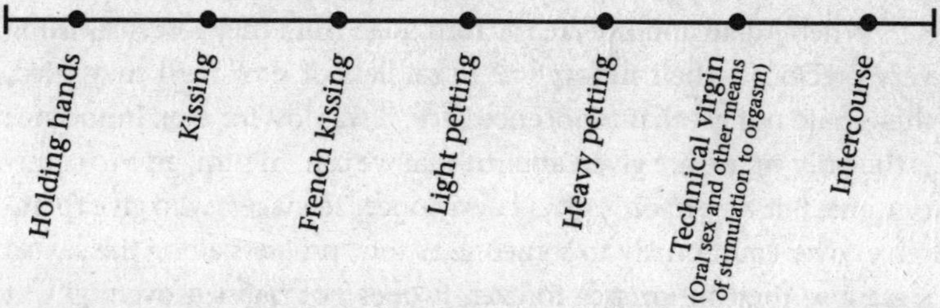

Light petting is generally defined as caressing someone from the waist up. Heavy petting is caressing from the waist down. But petting can have many different expressions:

- Hugging so that your hands caress your partner's back and sides
- Touching breasts and groin through or under clothing
- Lying down together or on top of each other
- Touching sexual organs in order to reach orgasm[4]

Petting is popular among teenagers. The Barna group released a survey on church youth in the US:

- 39 per cent of church youth see fondling breasts as acceptable
- 32 per cent see fondling genitals as acceptable
- 65 per cent have had some type of sexual contact, from fondling breasts to intercourse[5]

Many teenagers are also involved in oral sex. When I was a youth minister I was called to counsel a group of young people who had been to a masturbation party after school. They were just twelve years old! Today, because of AIDS and other sexually transmitted diseases, teenagers get involved in many sexual activities, but do not believe that they are involved in 'sex' because they have avoided intercourse. I call these students technical virgins because they have done everything sexual except the actual act of intercourse. They are definitely sexually active.

When Adam and Eve ate the forbidden fruit, they lost something very precious – their innocence. Regardless of how hard they tried, they could not get that innocence back, it was lost for ever. Innocence is the only *gift* we are given at birth that we can, in turn, give to someone else. But we can only give it away once. Teenagers who give themselves over emotionally to someone as they progress along the sexual scale lose their innocence forever. It does not happen overnight, it happens slowly. Starting with the act of cuddling, their innocence is stripped away with each move up the scale. By the time a person has reached the stage of technical virgin, they are no longer innocent or sexually pure. Even if they have not had intercourse, the damage has been done and they will be unable to give their spouse that gift of innocence. Today, Satan is waging an all-out attack to rob your children of their innocence, and he is willing to take it inch by inch.

My youngest son, Caleb, had a problem keeping his nappies on when he was a toddler. He would rip the tabs off and leave the nappy in the house when he went to play outside. He was known in our neighbourhood for being the boy who wore no pants. Jeremiah, being the understanding older brother, would shout at him and beg him to put his pants back on. But Caleb didn't see anything wrong with his lack of proper apparel. One day, Jeremiah stormed out of the house into the front garden where Caleb, pantless and happy, was playing. 'You're naked!' Jeremiah screamed at his little brother.

Caleb looked down at his bare body with horror on his little face, screamed and covered himself as he rushed inside. Suddenly, he was old enough to be embarrassed. He was no longer innocent. He would never again be comfortable being seen naked. That child-like innocence was gone, forever. Sexual innocence is the same. Once our children lose it, it can never be regained. And because it is so priceless, we must teach them to protect it.

What's the Problem With 'Going All the Way'?

My innocent hand-holding and peck-kissing with my first girlfriend Debbie was a part of the sexual progression. The desire for sex is like a powerful drug that entices us to keep coming back to it over and over again. But we must have bigger doses more often in order to receive the 'high' that we got that first time we held a hand or cuddled. When our children continue to progress up the scale, they may eventually reach the dead-end road that leads to intercourse. One teenager put it this way: 'Having premarital sex was the most horrifying experience of my life. It wasn't at all the emotionally satisfying or the casually-taken experience the world perceives it to be. I felt as if my insides were being exposed and my heart left unattended.'[6]

Where do you draw the line on the sexual progression scale? Most parents draw the line at holding hands (especially fathers of girls!). But most teenagers draw the line at oral sex. For twenty-five years I have been asking young people where they draw the line with the opposite sex and they tell me that anything is permissible as long as you don't go 'all the way'.

As we have seen, however, studies show that many of our young people are not drawing any lines. Many teenagers say that their bodies were designed for sex and that the desires have been placed within them, so what is the harm in fulfilling those desires?

The Bible tells us that God desires His children to view their bodies as holy. 'It is God's will that you should be sanctified: that you should avoid sexual immorality; that each of you should learn to control his own body in a way that is holy and honourable, not in passionate lust like the heathen' (1 Thessalonians 4:3–5 NIV). God is pleased and honoured when we offer our bodies to Him, pure and unstained. God wants our children to protect that sexual purity until the day they walk down the wedding aisle, because the consequences of premarital sex can haunt a young person for life.

Psychological consequences

I recall Pavlov's dogs from science studies. When he put food in a dog's bowl, he rang a bell. Soon, even without the food, the bell caused the dog to salivate. The bell related to food and it triggered a response. In the same way, when a teenager keeps having sexual encounters and knows he or she should not, the guilt inside goes off like a bell – a bell that will continue to ring even after marriage.

Nick and Mandy repeated their wedding vows in front of their family and friends and now they have a piece of paper that says they are legally married. They are both excited to be setting off on honeymoon, so amid the handfuls of confetti, they scurry out of the church and rush to a nearby hotel to begin their wedding night. Everything seems perfect. She emerges from the bathroom wearing the lingerie she purchased for this special occasion and he is ready and waiting on the bed. As they progress from cuddling to intercourse, both begin to hear a familiar bell ... guilt. Neither Nick nor Mandy are virgins. Both have had several partners before each other, and as they engage in marital sex, they are plagued by the guilt of premarital sex. Now, every time they enter the bed to make love, the familiar bell of guilt rings for both of them. Like Pavlov's dog, they have been conditioned to associate sex with guilt. For years, their lovemaking to each other as husband and wife will leave them feeling guilty.

Psychologists tell us that it takes ten years for a person who has had premarital sex to be able to engage in marital sex without guilt. Sadly, today, many marriages end in divorce before ten years, and the guilt starts all over again. Even sadder is the fact that premarital sex robs people of the ability to fully experience sex the way that God has designed it.

Physical consequences

Sexually transmitted diseases, AIDS, pregnancy and abortion can also be haunting reminders of going 'all the way'. Our teenagers are confronted by the glamour of sex, but they are rarely given the full story. Sex, society says, is a natural desire that should be fulfilled. The media makes hopping from bed to bed look like a recreational sport and never addresses the potential physical dangers involved in this type of lifestyle.

Spiritual consequences

Lisa and her boyfriend were both brought up in Christian homes where they had learned they should wait for marriage to have sex. They had heard from the 'old folks' that they would get carried away if they let their emotions get the best of them, but they both felt they could control their urges. After six months of going out together, they began to have sexual contact with each other, and a few months later they finally had intercourse.

At one time they had both been very close to God and had good relationships with Him, but their indulgence interfered terribly with that relationship. Whenever we disobey God, we fall out of fellowship with Him. Unless that relationship is restored through admitting our disobedience and accepting His forgiveness, we often continue making more disobedient choices. Those wrong choices always have consequences. For Lisa, the consequence was a deep sense of guilt and a poor relationship with her husband. The feelings of guilt have been there since they started going too far and they are still there.

Satan wants to rob our children of the purity that God desires for them and he is using everything he can get his hands on to launch this attack. Our teenagers are faced with incredible pressure to misuse the precious gift of sex for a cheap thrill. An evening in the back seat of a car can ruin a life forever. Having a girl- or boyfriend is an important issue during the teenage years and one that cannot be taken lightly.

How Young Is Too Young?

When Justin asked his father if he could take his girlfriend to the school sports tournament on Friday night, it seemed to be an innocent request. In fact, his father grinned and said, 'Well, Justin, I didn't know you had a girlfriend.' Justin nodded and told his father that he and Jenny had been going steady for three months. They had walked home from school together every day and sometimes did homework at each other's homes after school.

'Sounds pretty serious,' his father said. The smile had been replaced by a slight frown. Justin nodded again and said, 'Yeah. And I think it's time now to move on to proper dates. We're old enough now.' Justin was thirteen.

Justin's father had reason to be worried. He was concerned about two children as young as his son being out alone, as early dating could lead to early sex. Teenagers have natural desires that lead them to want to hold hands, cuddle, kiss and travel up the scale of sexual progression. Many teenagers see having a boy- or girlfriend as a way to explore the opposite sex and experiment with fulfilling some of the natural sexual desires within them. But going out with someone for these reasons leads our children to a very serious letdown: premarital sex.

God's Way

Going out on dates is a means to help us select a spouse, it is not a way to satisfy sexual desires. There are two important biblical principles that apply to doing this God's way. We need to communicate these principles to our children.

1. Go out with a believer

My wife and I are each moving towards God. As we move towards God, we move closer to one another. In our life, we have a common goal, to please and serve God:

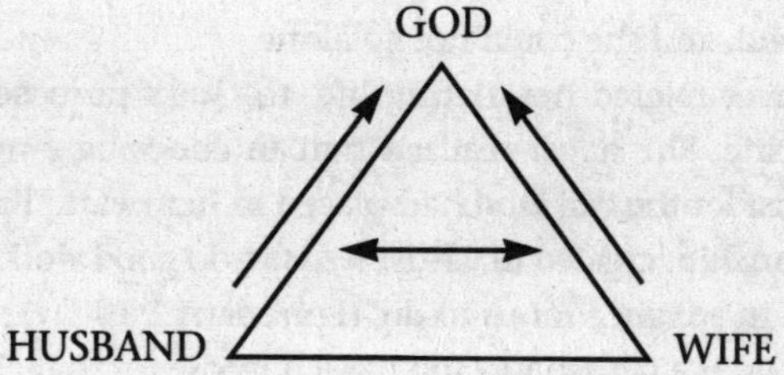

If your son or daughter is a Christian and is going out with a non-Christian, there are no spiritually significant common goals between them and they cannot move, spiritually, in a unified direction. 'Do not be yoked together with unbelievers. For what do righteousness and wickedness have in common? Or what fellowship can light have with darkness?' (2 Corinthians 6:14 NIV). Help your teenager understand the importance of viewing each person they go out with as a potential spouse. Ask them the question, 'If dating is the process to pick your mate, and if you wouldn't want to marry this person, why would you bother to go out with him/her?'

2. Link your choice of boy/girlfriend with God's purpose for your life

Seventeen-year-old Sherry was a girl in my youth group many years ago who felt God calling her to the mission field. We were all thrilled. Sherry was an energetic and intelligent young woman and we all agreed that she would be an excellent missionary. Sherry, however, began going out with a boy who had no desire to be a missionary. She was hanging on to him because she desperately wanted a boyfriend. It seemed as if all her dreams of going to the mission field were fading each day. I saw Sherry recently and as we began to talk, tears welled in her eyes. She still felt an intense desire to be a missionary. Nothing else that she did had given her the same fulfilment. Mission work, she said, was her passion, but she thought she would never be able to fulfil that call from God. She knew her husband would never go to the mission field, and she could not go alone.

Sherry never related her 'dating life' to God's purpose for the whole of her life. She never realized that in choosing a mate, she needed to consider the call God had placed in her heart. 'For we are God's workmanship, created in Christ Jesus to do good works, which God prepared in advance for us to do' (Ephesians 2:10 NIV).

If your child is a Christian, God has a purpose for that child that was determined before the creation of the world. Choosing a mate is a part of that purpose, and our children should bear this in mind when picking boy- and girlfriends.

When Jeremiah was fourteen, he came to me and said, 'Dad, I've made a decision. I'm going to keep myself pure until marriage.' He said he had also decided that finding a girlfriend was not a priority until he was ready to look seriously for a marriage partner. He had other goals in his life he wanted to pursue, and he did not want to complicate his life with a girlfriend. He has a lot of friends who are girls who call at our house and with whom he spends a lot of time in school and church activities. But he knows that a serious relationship takes time from other commitments, and has chosen to reserve that for another time later in life.

We want our children to make the right decisions, but we also want them to make those decisions for themselves. In the next chapter, we'll look at some ways we can contract with our children and help them set standards for boy/girlfriend relationships.

Thinking It Through

1. In Paul's letter to the Corinthians, he describes our bodies as temples of the Holy Spirit. How do you relate this in talking to your children about sex?
2. Are you helping your child view his/her body as a temple? How?
3. When you were going out with someone, where did you draw the line on the sexual progression scale? How have the choices you made back then affected you in your marriage and sex life?
4. What does your child see as the purpose of having a boy- or girlfriend? What words of wisdom would you give to your child about the benefits of following 'God's way'?

Getting a Grip

1. Sit down with your teenagers and search the Bible for verses about God's view of sex and our bodies. Some examples: 1 Thessalonians 4:3–6; Hebrews 13:4; 1 Corinthians 6:13; 1 Corinthians 6:18–20; Ephesians 5:3.
2. Show your teenagers the sexual progression scale and ask them where they would draw the line. Discuss why.
3. List for your teenagers the dangers of premarital sex and then discuss why God asks us to save intercourse until marriage.
4. Plan a conversation with your children about the 'right' age for having boy- and girlfriends. Discuss different options, such as group dates, double dates, single dates.

Chapter 7

It's More Than 'Just Say No'

I saw a cartoon recently that made me think carefully about the issue of communicating with our children about sex. A father entered his son's room with beads of nervous perspiration on his face and his hands shaking. The son was sitting on his bed and he looked up at his father innocently. 'Uh, son,' the nervous father said, wringing his hands, 'I came in to talk to you about something important.' The son looked up and set aside the book he was reading. 'Sure, Dad, come on in.'

The father walked in and stood at the foot of the bed and cleared his throat. There was a long pause and the son finally asked, 'Are you okay, Dad?' The father looked miserable. He finally blurted out the words, 'Do you know about girls and all that stuff because your mother told me if you didn't I needed to sit down and talk to you.'

The son smiled and picked up his book again, 'Dad, don't worry about a thing. I already know about all that.' The father looked relieved and turned to go. He gave his son a smile as he shut the door. After his father was gone, a girl peaked her head out from under the bed and said, 'Boy, that was close, you told me your parents never came home before five.'

As I pondered the dilemma of the poor father, I wondered how many parents out there are in the same situation. They are struggling to find a way to talk to their children about sex, but by the time they work up the courage, it's too late and their son or daughter has already been 'educated'. In a recent article, the American child support organization, Children Now, presented the following information: 'Most parents want to do their best in talking with their children about sex and sexuality. But they're often not sure how to begin. In fact, one of the most pressing questions on the minds of parents who want to talk with their children about sex is, "What should my child know and when should she know it?"' The article went on to list some excellent guidelines for parents wanting answers. Here's what the experts say:

- By the age of five, children should be familiar with the correct terms for sexual body parts, and how babies get in and out of a woman's body.
- By six to eight years old, children should be able to use biological terms – including vulva, vagina, breast, penis, scrotum and testicles – correctly and not have to rely on 'cute' family labels to talk about body parts.
- By nine to eleven years old, children should know that sexual feelings are normal and natural, the biological facts about how babies are born, including how the reproductive cycle works, and the physical and emotional changes girls and boys undergo in puberty.
- By twelve to thirteen years old, pre-teenagers should understand that sexual relationships bring pleasure as well as responsibility, that abstinence is a desirable alternative for young people, that teenage pregnancy and parenting often bring a loss of personal freedom and emotional, psychological and financial burdens. They should also know that you can prevent pregnancy with birth control, learn about different contraceptives, know what sexually transmitted diseases are and understand how they're transmitted, prevented and treated.[1]

For many parents, like the father I mentioned above, the very thought of approaching these issues with their children is overwhelming. However, the experts tell us it does not have to be. Just remember that effective parent-to-child sex education has four simple goals: (1) to provide accurate information; (2) to explain that sex is more than physical, and involves feelings and responsibilities; (3) to transmit your own family's values; and (4) to safeguard your children by laying a foundation that will help prevent risky behaviour later on.[2]

Our children are under enormous sexual pressure, both from their own bodies and from our permissive culture. At no time in history have there been creatures like the adolescents of today. They are going through puberty earlier and waiting longer and longer to get married. The time in between can be agonizing as they try to determine why they should and whether or not they will stay sexually pure. The urgency for timely, accurate, and effective communication about sex and sexuality has never been greater.

Unfortunately, parents seem to be hesitant to help their children if it means talking to them about sex. Researchers tell us that seven out of ten boys and three out of ten girls have never at any time been given advice about sex by their parents, even though teenagers prefer their parents as sexual advisors and information sources. Of those who were 'advised', more than two-thirds of the boys and a quarter of the girls felt that neither of their parents had helped them deal effectively with sex.[3]

Helping our children deal effectively with sex involves creating an atmosphere where open communication about any topic, including sex, is encouraged. We must also help our children set standards for their relationships so they will make their own decision to stay sexually pure until marriage.

Forget the Birds and the Bees

It is no surprise that teenagers are confused about sex. They are surrounded by conflicting messages. Their parents are warning them they had better not sleep around while the media tells them that sleeping around is the only way to have a good time.

Parents, it is vital that you regulate what your young children are seeing on television and at the cinema. As they get older, it is your responsibility to mediate what they see and hear by having open discussions with them.

In our society, if parents wait until their children have reached puberty to give them a one-time 'birds and the bees' talk, it may be too late. Like the father in the cartoon, we may be missing the truth of how much our children already know about sex. Real communication with our children is not a one-shot process, it must begin when our children are very young and continue on into adulthood.

Our family's Good Word/Bad Word project opened the door for us to talk about sex with our boys long before they reached adolescence. Homosexuality, abortion and AIDS were all words they brought home and placed on the chart. As we talked about these words, they began to ask questions that led to other questions and soon we were talking openly about sex. We gave them as much information as we felt they needed at each particular age. As they grew older, the information that we gave them when we talked about these words helped them make decisions about sex for themselves. It gave us the perfect opportunity to discuss the how, what and why of sexual issues.

Many parents withhold information about sex until their children are teenagers. Then they sit down with them for a tense sex talk where they dump all of this information on them at once. But if children have received little or no information about sex, this sudden waterfall of facts is overwhelming. And many times, as the cartoon shows, it is already too late.

Children are natural observers and persistent question-askers. They are constantly studying the world around them and trying to put it all together. If we give them the opportunity, they will present us with many occasions to communicate about sex. What child hasn't asked the question, Where do babies come from? Josh McDowell gives wise guidelines for communicating with our children about sex:

> When it comes to specifically what we should teach our children and at what ages, the operative principle is that little questions

> deserve little answers; big questions deserve big answers, and frank questions deserve frank answers. Tailor what you teach, in other words, to the age and actual question of the child. Loading down a child with too much information too soon can cause confusion and anxiety.[4]

To illustrate this principle, consider the following anecdote. A five-year-old child asked, 'Dad, what's sex?' Dad took a deep breath and delivered The Big Talk. The child took an identification card out of his new wallet. 'So, Dad,' he asked, 'do I write "M" or "F"?' When it needs to be simple, just keep it simple.

> The same thing (simplicity principle) applies to non-sexual questions. How does a car go? You put gasoline into the fuel tank and the gas works inside the engine to make the car go. The child is not asking about combustion engines ... Parents are nervous. When you talk about sex, your own attitudes are on the line. In parenting, you learn as you go along. You have to grow into a comfort with the subject.[5]

If your children are older and you have neglected this area of parenting, remember: it is never too late to start. If you have been discussing issues of sexuality with small children in your family, keep in mind that the content of such discussions needs to change as they get older. Here are a few tips for talking to older children and teenagers:

- Go beyond the facts. Talk about values, including responsibility, respect, privacy and commitment. Stress relationships, rather than sex, as the goal.
- As children become teenagers, shift gears from being available, to influencing and directing. Teach your teenager how to make decisions.
- Give teenagers information about sexual responsibility, contraception and sexually transmitted diseases. Depending on your religious outlook, share your views on abstinence or 'safe sex'.
- Don't be afraid to make mistakes. There will be opportunities to clarify your views in the next conversation.[6]

Open the door every day for communication about sex to your children and look for opportunities to help them get a grip on sexual values, before sexual activity gets a grip on them.

If your children are going to be able to make healthy, moral choices about their sexuality throughout their lives they must continually be encouraged to ask parents and other trusted adults for information. When it comes to sex education, be a resource, not a recluse, as their parent.

Contracting: A Foundation for Dating

Going out on dates is like driving: it's best to know the rules of the road before you get behind the wheel. The 'dating contract' is like the written portion of the driving test. Before a teenager rushes out for that first date, he should have taken the time to write out his standards. Then he is ready for the actual road test: the date. (Maybe every country should have a Department of Dating that makes sure you can pass the test before you make the date!)

It can also be a scary process for parents. After many years of nurturing your children and praying for their sexual purity, they finally arrive at the stage of life where they are old enough to leave after dark with someone of the opposite sex. Suddenly, we are standing at the door trying to wave goodbye and point at our watch at the same time while shouting, 'Remember! Back by ten o'clock!' And what parent hasn't waited by the door at ten o'clock, trying desperately to look nonchalant as their teenager strolls in. 'So what did you do?' we ask, as if we really expect them to sit down and tell us. They usually shrug and say, 'You know, this and that.'

Going out on a date is a rite of passage in a young person's life. It is a defining moment and should not be left to chance. As we stand at the door and wave goodbye, we need the assurance that our children have been given both information and standards. 'Children, obey your parents in the Lord, for this is right' (Ephesians 6:1 NIV). 'Children, obey your parents in everything, for this pleases the Lord' (Colossians

3:20 NIV). While these verses state the responsibility of the child, implied is the duty of the parents to provide information and standards.

As your children reach 'dating age', it becomes increasingly important that they are given guidance in setting standards of behaviour for maintaining relationships with members of the opposite sex. They need to know clearly what you expect, and what the Bible expects. Before a child reaches this age, parents should sit down with him or her and help create a 'dating contract'. The contract allows parents and children to talk openly about the issues of setting standards for relationships. Each contract should include the reasons why the child has decided not to have premarital sex, a list of standards to be kept while out on a date and the consequences of compromising the standards. Once again, the child is given the opportunity to assign values to certain actions. If the child has helped put the standards in place, he or she will be much more likely to follow the standards.

There are several things you and your children need to do before creating this contract.

1. Talk openly about sex

A dating contract will be useless if your teenager does not have the information they need to make a decision about their sexual purity. They need to know the purpose of marital sex, and the dangers of casual sex. They also need to feel comfortable talking about sex. It should not be viewed by the family as a subject that is off limits or so embarrassing that it cannot be discussed above a whisper. Sex is a natural part of life and should be open for discussion.

2. Search the Scriptures

God created sex, so He should have the final word on how it is to be used. The Bible is filled with stories of people who paid a price for sexual impurity: Noah's son, Samson, Solomon, David, Bathsheba, the Samaritan woman at the well. Encourage your children to read Song of Songs also, a book that shows the importance of sex in a marital relationship, and then read 1 Corinthians, a letter Paul wrote to a church that had forgotten about sexual purity. Also, see 1 Thessalonians 4, Hebrews 13 and Ephesians 5.

3. Talk openly about dating

Find out from your teenagers their views on the purpose of having boy- or girlfriends and then allow them to think about what their standards for such relationships should be. Don't impose all of your standards on them. Give them the opportunity to think about the standards they would like to put in the contract, then sit down and write the contract together.

Putting It on Paper: Ideas for a Dating Contract

Every contract will look different, but there are certain standards that should be discussed with your teenager and then included in the contract. Here are a few ideas.

1. How far can I go on a date before it is a sin?

The child must decide where he or she will draw the line. Before that first date, they should have written into the contract how far they can go and why. If the child determines it is okay to French kiss on a date, they need to write out why.

2. The logical consequences of 'going all the way'

What are the physical, emotional, mental and spiritual consequences of not waiting for sex? Get your teenager to include these consequences in the contract.

3. The benefits of waiting for marital sex

As teenagers write the benefits of following God's standards for sex, they are able to see on paper the results of both choices. They begin to make an evaluation for themselves about which choice they will make. These benefits should also be included in the contract.

4. I will respect the person I go out with

'Love is patient...' (1 Corinthians 13:4 NIV). Love and respect go hand in hand. If we love and respect the person we go out with, then we want what is best for them. We don't want to cause them to stumble. Premarital sex always causes a person to stumble. It leaves scars that do not heal quickly. If we respect the person we go out with, we want to show them love, and love is patient.

5. I will go out with someone who is in harmony with their parents

One of the Ten Commandments says, 'Honour thy father and mother.' Teenagers who are rebelling against authority are more likely to involve themselves in reckless behaviour, including pre-marital sex.

6. I will wait for God's timing

Having a boy- or girlfriend is not a hobby. It is a process of searching for the person God has chosen for us. To know God's timing we must be willing to listen to Him. Being involved in a relationship can take away from other activities or plans that God has in mind. If it seems to be getting in the way of other important pursuits, it may need to be put on hold.

7. I will go out with people God has put in my life for a purpose.

Every person we go out with will either build us up or tear us down. Not a single date will leave us neutral. God's will is that we find someone who will encourage and build us up in the kingdom of God and He will place people in our lives to fulfil that purpose. Bible teacher John McArthur says that to find the right person one must first be the right person.

8. If the person I want to go out with does not fit the standards I have set, I will not get involved.

He may be the perfect dream date. She may be the most beautiful and popular girl. But if he's rebellious, or if she is not willing to wait for sex until marriage, then the relationship is off. God will bring into your child's life a person whom God will use to fulfil the standards in his or her dating contract. Encourage him or her to wait until that person is found.

9. If I get stuck on a 'bad date' I will ...

Every teenager needs to have a plan. Your teenager needs to be able to tell you what he will do if he is on a date that starts to get too hot and heavy. When my boys were little, I would practise with them the skill of saying 'NO!' I would dress up as a stranger and ask them to go with me. I taught them to turn round and scream 'NO!' Our teenagers need to learn to say this word. And they need to write out a course of action they will take to end a bad date.

I talked to a teenager the other day who has a rather drastic plan. As soon as she gets in the car with her new date, she tells him, 'You'd like my dad. He has this great gun collection. By the way, he has this idea that I'm his little princess and boy does he get upset if someone mistreats his little princess.' Talk about an intimidating way to start a date! One of the simplest and most effective action plans is to teach your child just to say 'No!' A mobile phone is another possible tool to provide for your child to use if anything begins to get out of hand.

We teach children what to do when there's a fire. We teach them what to say if someone tries to abduct them. But we send them off on a date, hormones and all, with no plan of action. Help your teenager come up with a plan, and encourage him or her to stick with it.

Keep the contract in a place where both you and your teenager can review it. It's easy to relax the standards if the contract sits in a drawer and is never seen again. Give your children the tools they need to face a world where sex is unholy and then send them out with the faith that God will bless their relationships if they are totally committed to Him. It has been my experience that when a dating contract is used, teenagers have a much higher sense of integrity and the values involved, and seldom fail to live up to the standards that they have set for themselves.

Thinking It Through

1. If you have not had open communication with your child about sex, how much do you think he or she knows about it? From what source do you think he or she is learning about sex?
2. What kind of sex education did you receive as a child? If your childhood family was uncomfortable discussing sex, how have you carried that uneasiness over into your family?
3. Can you tell the difference between your child's little questions, big questions and frank questions enough to know how to answer?
4. On a scale of 1–10, how comfortable are you sending your child out on a date?

Getting a Grip

1. Write down common questions children ask about sex, such as, Where do babies come from? and What does sex mean? Then write down answers to these questions that are appropriate to the age of your children. Be prepared to answer these questions when they are asked!
2. Sit down with your teenager and have her write out her idea of the 'perfect date'. Talk with her about the qualities that are important to her in a date or a relationship.
3. Prepare to create a dating contract with your child by spending several nights searching the Scriptures together. End with Paul's first letter to the Corinthians, and discuss why God put standards in place for sex.
4. In the US there is a growing 'True Love Waits' campaign for teenagers and there is no reason why the principles cannot be applied in other countries too. At the end of the programme, each young person is required to sign a pledge card, committing themselves to sexual abstinence before marriage.

Part IV

You Want to Pierce What?

Getting a Grip On Communicating With Your Child

Chapter 8

The Missing Links of Communication

'My daughter is sixteen and I can't remember the last time we sat down and had a decent conversation.' 'When I ask my son how his day was at school, he shrugs, stares at me blankly, and then shuts himself in his room for the rest of the day.'

'We tried to take a family holiday last year and our kids spent the whole time with headphones stuck to their ears, trying to ignore us.' 'My daughter walked in the other day and announced to her father and me that she wanted to get her lip pierced. We almost fell off our chairs.'

Parents are struggling to understand and communicate with their teenage children. It's a fact of life: the gap between generations makes it hard for both parents and children to meet in the middle. Many young people do not feel that they are able to relate to their parents, and many parents are uncomfortable trying to relate to their children. Therefore, accomplishing any meaningful communication sometimes seems like an awesome task for everyone.

Despite the fact that we now live in what has been termed the 'information age', our society struggles with the growing inability of people to communicate with each other. We are uncomfortable if we are trapped in lifts with people we don't know, so we keep our eyes glued to the floor to avoid looking at the faces of the people standing twelve inches away from us. If one poor soul does get the bright idea to start a conversation, the discussion is usually awkward and ends abruptly, and thankfully, when the lift door opens.

Many of us live only a few feet from neighbours, but our relationships are reduced to quick waves as we rush in and out of our driveways. No longer do we need our neighbours, as we once did, for survival, but rather we cocoon ourselves in our homes and hardly know the people who live around us. Conversations are often reduced to exchanging voice mails or using our computers to send e-mail. And families are so busy that sitting down and having a conversation at the dinner table has been replaced by hastily scrawled notes left on the kitchen counter: *Leftover pizza is in the freezer. Had a meeting at six, Johnny won't be home until eight. See you around nine.*

Educationalist Stephen Glenn makes this point:

> In an earlier era, communicating was easier simply because there was nothing else to do. Large families gathered together in the evening without a television and shared the details of the day. Today, we gather around our television sets to spend the evening 'together' as a family. If work time, travel time to and from work, sleep time, and viewing time average 23 hours of the day in a family, there is just one hour in twenty-four left for family interaction. This leaves out mealtimes and the normal business of the family. But ... mealtime and viewing time could be combined. Of course, this is done at the expense of all the discussion and sharing that used to take place at the dinner table ... In less than thirty years we have gone from a society with a surplus of significant interactions between the generations, particularly within the primary family unit, to a society in which there is a critical shortage of that kind of significant interaction.[1]

It's no surprise that we complain about the lack of communication in our families. Our children are learning how to tune out the world, and in the process they are tuning out their families. As our society grows increasingly individualistic, parents need to rediscover three keys to effective communication: grandparents, time and perception.

The Grandparent Factor

Every home needs law *and* grace. As parents, we see our role as the law – what we say goes: 'Pick up your toys!' 'Sit down!' 'Don't talk with your mouth full!' But we also know that we need to give grace to our children – offering a sympathetic ear for their explanations, forgiving, and wiping the slate clean. It is a delicate balancing act and we often tip the scales with too much law. After all, it's hard to listen gently and quietly to a child's explanation for breaking a priceless family heirloom. Punishment, we say, must be swift and severe so the child will learn! But that child also needs affirmation and understanding, something that is hard to give in a moment of anger.

Grandparents can provide grace for children, a place of comfort and release. Let's travel back to the Waltons once again. It is a hot summer evening and John Boy's father is angry. The two of them stand at the top of the stairs, the father lecturing loudly while his son cowers near the wall. 'If I ever see you do anything like that again I'll tan your hide!' the father shouts and stomps down the stairs and out of the front door. John Boy stands at the top of the stairs for a few minutes, his shoulders slumped, and his eyes filling with tears. Finally, he slowly trudges down the stairs and sits down at the kitchen table. In a matter of seconds, Grandpa sits down beside him and wraps his arms around his grandson.

John Boy buries his head in Grandpa's shoulder and sobs for a while, then begins to pour his heart out. Grandpa listens, then begins to tell stories about John Boy's father. 'He made mistakes too, you know,' he says with a smile. John Boy's grandfather offers his grandson a much needed moment of grace. John Boy learns that his father is human, and perhaps it makes the angry lecture he received seem a little less painful.

Grandparents offer the grace that is very often missing from today's families. They have the time to listen, to explain, and to affirm the child's self-worth when the parents cannot, and this is crucial. If a child lives in an environment where there is only law, you can be sure he has rebellion simmering beneath the surface. The child may be 'kept in line' for a period of time, but he is simply waiting for his opportunity to get back at the authoritarian ruling he has been living under. Grandparents give a balance that so many families today need. But where are the grandparents, now that we parents need them more than ever? Glenn says, for example, 'In 1840 approximately 60 to 70 per cent of all households in America had at least one grandparent as a full-time active member of the household. Today less than 2 per cent have a grandparent available as a resource.'[2]

In the days when grandparents and extended families lived together or very near each other, most of the time a child was conversing with someone older or younger than himself. The child's life was filled with intergenerational association. They learned skills and knowledge from the older generations, and they learned how to express ideas and thoughts for the younger children.

When I was a child, I went to a school with two grades in one room. It was a great way to learn communication skills, because when it was time for our lesson, we scooted our chairs up to the teacher's desk and we interacted with her. She asked us questions, and we were able to seek and discuss answers. Many times we were called upon to help the younger pupils with their lessons. We scooted our chairs over to their row and helped them with their studies. In a typical day, we were offered opportunities to communicate concepts, skills and ideas with people who were both older and younger than ourselves.

Children don't have as much access to intergenerational association today because many grandparents and extended family members don't live nearby. Also, the roles of grandparents today are different from what they were many years ago. Grandma and Grandpa are often much more mobile and independent, living apart from the rest of the family and travelling off on leisurely holidays, 'making the most' of their retirement years.

What to Do if You Don't Have Grandparents Available

Without the chance to spend time with different generations, children fail to learn important communication skills and they miss out on the grace-filled relationships that many grandparents offer. Since we live a long way from our children's grandparents, we decided to 'adopt' grandparents. We chose two older adults in our church with whom we already had a relationship. These two dear people fulfilled the role of grandparents for our boys in every way. They helped us celebrate birthdays, took part in special school events, and spent time affirming and communicating with Jeremiah and Caleb.

When one of my sons was seventeen, he was going through a tough time as he tried to figure out what to do with his life after leaving school. So he hopped into the car and drove over to 'Grandma's' house, sat in her living room, and cried his eyes out. She was there to listen to his frustrations, and then affirm him as a person. Although Cathy and I had been actively doing both of those things, there is something special about Grandma. She has the ability to listen without feeling the urge to give out an armload of advice. And she cheers him on with the eagerness of someone who is not on his team simply because she has to be.

These days many parents are so busy and stressed out at the end of the day that their only communication with their children is to bark orders: 'Get your homework done!' 'Clean up this mess!' 'Get ready for bed, you've got to get up early tomorrow!' We are missing the moments of quiet, natural conversation which emerge when someone is willing to take the time to sit down and listen. Children have a lot to tell us, but more often than not we can't find the time to listen. We need another set of ears to help us.

It is important for our children to learn to communicate with and understand someone much older than themselves. That older 'grace-giver' may indeed be a grandparent, but very often is not an immediate family member. And regardless of the role that older person may play in the life of your child, it is important that children learn to understand and communicate with older adults. When I was a youth minister, our teenagers learned firsthand what it felt like to be a senior citizen. The week before Valentine's Day we held a four-hour session on a Sunday in which the young people 'aged' by about sixty years. We called it 'The Experiment in Ageing'.

First, we covered their eyes with a double layer of gauze so they could experience deteriorating vision. On their hands they wore large plastic bags, fastened tightly at the wrists so that blood flow was diminished, which affected dexterity and caused the hands to sweat and ache. We tied a piece of sturdy rope around their legs so they could only move their feet about six inches apart. Suddenly these vibrant, active teenagers were transformed into a group of people who shuffled through the halls of our church with their necks protruding like tortoises, trying to focus their eyes through the heavy gauze. Gripping doorknobs was a challenge, but nothing compared to trying to turn the pages in the hymnbook during church! Since the youth choir was scheduled to sing that night, it was a perfect opportunity for them to learn to negotiate the choir loft stairs with their 'arthritic' legs. They sang a beautiful song from memory, then slowly descended the stairs. The experiment was wearing thin.

After sitting through a sermon with achy hands, almost-blind eyes, and legs that could hardly move, they were anxious for the service to end. They shuffled back to the youth room and tore off their garb. At first it had been a fun experience, but by the time it was over they were ready to have their bodies back.

On the Monday after our experiment, the young people delivered flowers and spent some time with the senior citizens in the church. I remember a young girl named Molly who was visiting one of our older members at a nursing home. When Molly reached down to shake her hand, the older lady told her to be careful because she had arthritis. 'Oh I know,' Molly replied. 'I had it yesterday and it *hurts*.' Communication is more than words, it is understanding. Now Molly understood this older lady sitting in front of her and they began to interact with and learn from each other. Children need to learn that older adults can be a valuable resource for wisdom, encouragement, and affirmation in their lives. As your children develop skill in relating to and communicating with older adults, they will more readily accept the counsel of those 'grace-givers' in their life.

Parents, if your children don't have the blessing of being near their grandparents, find an older adult who will take the time to 'grandparent' your children. There are many older people who are not living near their grandchildren and who would be delighted to fulfil that role for your children. Take advantage of that opportunity to open up new doors of communication for your family.

The Time Factor

If I had to spell the word *love*, I might not spell it L-O-V-E. As a parent, I have realized that love also means T-I-M-E. One of the missing links of communication involves the time we spend with our children.

We are always communicating to our children, even when we don't realize it. A father who spends all of his time at the office and doesn't participate in the lives of his children is communicating this message loud and clear: *I don't have time for you. There are other things in my life that are more important.* A mother who spends all of the time she has with her children nagging and yelling at them sends this message: *You are a nuisance and a bother. I can't find anything I like about you.*

Communicating is more than talking. It is actions, also. We can say words over and over to our children, but unless we back those words up with actions, they are meaningless. We tell our children that they are important to us and we love being with them, but if we are so busy that we can't make the time to be with them, we are communicating a very different message. Former pastor and successful seminar presenter Dr John Maxwell has a life principle to remember: You teach what you know, you reproduce what you are. Make no mistake about it, your children know the difference between your 'talk' and your 'walk'.

When I was a youth minister, I used to make visits during the week. One evening as I was leaving, eight-year-old Caleb stood by the door and asked me where I was headed. 'I'm going out to tell people about Jesus,' I replied, hoping he would realize what an important task his father was about to undertake. He looked up at me and said, 'Why don't you stay home and tell us about Jesus?' Caleb's question made me realize that I had an important task at home that I could not afford to neglect. So every Monday night, one of my 'visits' was to my own home where I sat and talked to my boys about Jesus. Then I would go and make the rest of the visits.

During Jesus' ministry, people tugged at Him from all directions. There were so many people who needed His healing touch or to hear His teachings. The disciples were constantly amazed at the crowds that gathered to present their needs to Him. On one particular occasion, in the midst of healing and teaching, Jesus took an opportunity to teach an important lesson about time.

> People were bringing little children to Jesus to have him touch them, but the disciples rebuked them. When Jesus saw this, he was indignant. He said to them, 'Let the little children come to me, and do not hinder them, for the kingdom of God belongs to such as these. I tell you the truth, anyone who will not receive the kingdom of God like a little child will never enter it.' And he took the children in his arms, put his hands on them and blessed them.
>
> (Mark 10:13–16 NIV)

In front of the crowds of people, Jesus stopped what He was doing and received the children. The Scripture makes it clear that Jesus did not just make a hurried dash through the crowd of children, patting their heads as He passed. Instead, He took the children in His arms. He made sure they knew at that moment that there was nothing more important to Him than spending time with them.

In a world that is cold and impersonal, children need all the time we can give them. Quality time is quantity time. Paul Faulkner, in his wonderful book *Raising Faithful Children in a Fast-Paced World* says, 'The concept of quality time has been vastly overrated. It seems to carry the idea of doing as much as you can as quickly as you can. But what children need is a relaxed, spontaneous, unrushed atmosphere.'[3] A friend who was visiting our house once asked Caleb this question, 'How do you know your dad loves you?' Caleb's face broke into a wide grin and he answered, 'Because he wrestles with me.'

Our time with our children does not require an agenda. We don't have to provide them with a 'to do' list of activities or a calendar of entertaining events. In fact, some of the deepest conversations I've had with my sons have been during unstructured time, when we were relaxed and there was nothing scheduled. In our society, we admire productivity; in fact, many of us are uncomfortable if we spend time that is unproductive. But don't be afraid to 'waste' an afternoon just hanging out with your children. Give them an opportunity to share their hearts, and then give yourself the opportunity to listen.

Beware of blocking communication with your children by building walls. As parents we waste a lot of time building walls when we could be building relationships. This is especially true when our children are teenagers. When my oldest son was thirteen, we were getting ready for church one Sunday morning and Jeremiah came out of his room, ready for church. I glanced at him and immediately noticed that he wasn't wearing socks. 'You forgot something,' I said, motioning towards his feet.

He looked at me blankly and said, 'I'm dressed. I've got my shirt on, and my trousers on, and my shoes on.'

'But no socks,' I said quickly as I started to walk out of the door. 'Go and put your socks on,' I said over my shoulder.

'I can't,' he said.

I stopped and turned around. 'Why not?' I asked.

'I can't tell you.'

'Come on, Jeremiah, you can tell me. I'm a youth minister. I understand these things.'

'No, Dad. You wouldn't understand.'

'Come on, son, give me a chance.'

Jeremiah cleared his throat and said softly, 'They hurt my feet.'

'What?' I roared. 'Socks hurt your feet? Everybody wears socks. Your grandfather wore socks, I wear socks, your little brother wears socks. We all wear socks. No one has ever complained that their feet hurt from socks. I've never heard anything ...' I stopped. Suddenly, I looked at my sockless son and realized that this was a battle I didn't need to fight. Of course socks didn't hurt my son's feet. He was not telling me that socks hurt his feet, he was telling me they hurt his standing with his peer group. For him to fit in with the group he went around with at church, he had to get rid of the socks.

He was standing in front of me, waiting for me to finish my tirade. 'I guess socks could hurt your feet,' I said. 'I've never had any socks that hurt my feet, but it's not impossible. Let's go to church. Forget the socks.'

And he did forget the socks, but only for about a month. Then he was wearing socks again. But I could have taken that incident and let it drive a wedge between my son and me. We would have battled over something as insignificant as socks. How many times do we choose to spend our time battling the insignificant with our children? So what if their trousers are a little baggy, or their hair is a little longer? Let's spend time with our children building relationships instead of battling it out with them over things that don't matter. Trust me, you will have plenty of opportunities to go into battle over things that do matter. Jay Kessler, president of Youth for Christ/USA, says:

> When I say, 'Don't sweat the small stuff,' or 'Major on the majors, not on the minors,' you may ask, 'Well what *are* some of the minors

and majors?' The 'minors' are things like clothing, music, hairstyles, food preferences and messy rooms. With a little bit of obligatory nagging by parents, most young people will 'shape up' in these areas – eventually. 'Negative' tastes are probably not going to stay with them the rest of their lives or affect them permanently.[4]

What are the 'majors'? They will be different for each family, according to your own value system. As a general rule of thumb, you might consider majors to be any activity that is unbiblical or illegal, for example, drug use or under legal age consumption of alcohol. Or, it may be something that you think has the potential to jeopardize the health or well-being of your child. It may be something about which you know your wisdom is superior to your child's as it relates to consequences or long-term effects. An example might be dealing with your child's desire to have a tattoo or pierce their tongue. You need to remember that if you constantly reject everything that your child stands for, they may not view their relationship with you as 'safe' enough if they ever are faced with serious trouble.

We can waste precious months or even years not taking the time to get to know our children. Jeremiah's favourite baseball player is New York Yankees player Don Mattingly. When he was a young boy he collected Mattingly's baseball cards, posters and magazines with articles and pictures of him. Everyone in our family knew that Jeremiah was Mattingly's number one fan.

One day Caleb came screaming and crying to me that Jeremiah had torn up one of his favourite books, so I rushed to my older son's bedroom where he was sitting on his bed. 'Did you do this?' I asked, waving the torn book in front of him. He nodded guiltily so I picked up one of his Don Mattingly magazines. 'I'm going to teach you a lesson about how it feels to have someone destroy your property,' I said as I began to tear up the magazine. 'Do you know why Don Mattingly is my favourite baseball player?' he asked in a small voice. I shook my head. 'Because he looks like you,' he said sincerely.

I stopped and looked into his eyes. Then I looked at one of the Mattingly posters on his wall. 'You never told me that,' I said and sat down on his bed, still holding the magazine. He shrugged. I realized that perhaps I had not spent enough time with my son to find out *why* this baseball player meant so much to him.

Love is a four letter word spelled T-I-M-E, and it is a key to successful communication with our children.

The Perception Factor

I was out shopping not long ago and saw a sign that read: 'Ears Pierced, Half Off'. I had to stop and read it again to make sure it wasn't saying what I thought it said. Some people might hesitate to go in the shop for fear that they would come out with half their ears gone!

Sometimes, we communicate with our children based on *our* perception alone. The person who wrote the ear-piercing sign knew what they were trying to communicate, but they didn't stop to think how it might sound to the person walking by.

For example, you say to your seven-year-old child, 'Tidy your room,' so he goes to tidy his room. Probably, each of you has a different perception of 'tidy'. Your perception is based on many years of tidying rooms and seeing tidied rooms. So your expectations will be high. Your child's perception of tidy will be different, maybe just a pathway cleared so that they can walk to the wardrobe.

So the child 'tidies' the room and calls you in for an inspection. You look around at the pile of clothes stashed in the corner, the books stacked on the chest of drawers, and the toys that have been relocated from one side of the room to the other.

'You call this tidy?' you shout.

He looks around and nods his head, 'This is tidy.'

And it probably is, in your child's perception of a tidy room.

It is not always easy to see things from someone else's viewpoint. We are used to forming our own perceptions and holding tightly to them. This fact is always evident to me when I read a book, then see the film. When I am reading the book, I form a picture in my mind of the hero. As I continue to read, my mind keeps on drawing a picture of this hero, until the details are filled in and I know exactly what he looks like. I have my own perception of the hero. Then I go to see the film and at once I realize that somebody else's perception was different from mine. Since I like my perception better, I don't enjoy the film as much. This isn't my hero, this is somebody else's hero.

As adults and parents, we have formed many perceptions over the years and we find it difficult to look at things through the eyes of someone else – especially our children. We are sure that their perception should be exactly like ours! But when we practise looking at the world through the eyes of our children, we are able to understand and relate to them on a different level. Our communication grows and deepens. We are communicating more clearly with them. Suddenly, we understand why they don't want to wear socks, or why their room doesn't look picture-perfect tidy like we expected. We decided in our home many years ago that if we asked our boys to tidy their rooms, then we had to define what we meant: tidy is clothes in the drawers or laundry basket, the bed made, the toys in the toy box, and the shoes on the shoe rack. So when the boys are asked to tidy their room, everybody has the same perception of what that means.

Perception is also listening. It's realizing that there may be more to what our children are saying than what is heard on the surface. Communication is not just words, it is also understanding who someone is. When I understand that my six-year-old is not an adult, but a child who has limited life experience of being in dark rooms, I can begin to communicate with him about his fear of the dark. I don't expect him to behave like an adult and drift off to sleep when the lights are turned out. I understand his perception that the wardrobe seems like a perfect place for monsters to hide at night. And I understand my thirteen-year-old's perception that being accepted by his peer group is more important than wearing socks.

Jesus was a master at affirming the self-worth of people. Whether He was talking to a prostitute, an elite religious leader, a leper, a young rich kid, or a small child, He knew how to affirm them and let them know how much they were loved by God. He had perfect communication skills.

The way we communicate to our children either builds their self-esteem or tears it down. We must make it a priority to spend time with our children, listening to them, answering their questions, and developing natural communication. We must also see things from their perspective and provide them with the opportunities to develop family relationships with grandparents. As we do this, we will begin to provide our children with the kind of communication they need to affirm their self-worth.

Thinking It Through

1. When there is so much information available, and so many technological ways to communicate, why do you think people find it harder and harder to communicate with each other?
2. How much time do your children spend interacting with people who are older or younger? In what ways do you think this interaction helps them learn communication skills?
3. Do you provide your children with law *and* grace? Is your home balanced between the two, or are your children given rules without explanations?
4. What do your words communicate to your children? Do your actions communicate something different?
5. Is it difficult for you to spend time with your children that is unstructured? Why?
6. What are some ways you can improve the understanding factor in your home? Do you find yourself expecting more of your children than they understand? What does this have to do with perception?

Getting a Grip

1. If your child spends time with his grandparents, ask him, 'What is the best thing about Grandma and/or Grandpa?' The answer might surprise you!
2. Get together with your children's grandparents and talk about a time during the week that can be set aside as 'grandparent time'. Write it on the calendar and make it a priority.
3. Reduce the amount of structured activities for your younger children so you can spend more 'wasted time' with them.
4. In the midst of conflict with your children, stop and ask yourself if you are perceiving the situation from your eyes or theirs.
5. Make sure the perception of any task is clear to both child and parent.

Chapter 9

Learn to Affirm

Every parent remembers their child's first step. For months the anxious parents have watched their baby's chubby legs buckle and collapse before he could place one foot in front of the other. Finally, when the parents are least expecting it, baby slowly takes one or two steps, speeding up just in time to fall forward into Mum's or Dad's arms.

With unrestrained enthusiasm, the parents cheer wildly. 'You did it!' they shout as they hug and cuddle baby. Now the job of coaxing baby to continue this process called walking begins. Even after each tumble, when baby has fallen back on his bottom, the parents continue to applaud. 'Good job!' they say, clapping and smiling.

I can remember when my boys were learning to walk. Cathy and I were like noisy cheerleaders as we watched them toddle, fall, then pull themselves back up. 'Way to go!' 'Good job!' 'You can do it!' We rooted for them as we brushed away their tears.

We would never have considered giving up on them. We never threw up our hands in disgust and said, 'Can't you do anything right? You're never going to learn to walk if you don't concentrate. Now come on, shape up, and put those legs to work. What's the matter with you?'

We believed in our boys. We knew that they would learn to walk and we knew our job was to communicate that belief to them. Even if no one else believed those chubby little legs would someday be darting through our house at breakneck speed, we believed it.

But somehow, between the age of twelve months and the teenage years, parents find that being a cheerleader gets tougher. Our applause is sometimes lost in the day-to-day struggles that we encounter with our children. After all, it's hard to clap when you're holding a bad report card. And it's hard to cheer when your teenager is locked in the bedroom with his stereo blasting.

And as the years go by, we're tempted to get a little lazy. The affirming words take more effort than the nagging lectures. It's easier to say, 'I told you so,' than it is to say, 'What can I help you do to fix this problem?'

The Bible gives us clear direction on how important affirmation is: 'Therefore encourage one another and build each other up, just as in fact you are doing' (1 Thessalonians 5:11 NIV). Affirmation is vital to children. They need to hear more positives than negatives. When we learn to affirm our children's worth through the way we communicate with them, we are helping them become godly men and women. But affirmation takes effort, commitment and an understanding of the positive effects it has on our children.

The Chequebook Theory for Raising Children

My wife keeps the chequebook in our family. She understands the logical consequences of letting me loose with it – more withdrawals than deposits. I might take out more money than I was putting in and eventually there would be nothing left to withdraw from. The account would be empty.

The same principle applies to the chequebook theory of parenting: you cannot make withdrawals without first making deposits. The deposits are the loving expressions of affirmation we should give our children each day. Every time we give our children affirmation, whether it is a simple 'I love you', or taking the time to listen to a problem and express concern, we are making a deposit into their 'account'. Every day we can deposit love, acceptance, good thoughts and positive emotions into our children. As we continue to make these deposits, their account grows 'richer' and they are more prepared to tackle a negative world. The withdrawals come in many forms.

1. Nagging

Many parents waste communication opportunities by using their time to berate or lecture their children about shortcomings. Admittedly, there are times when children need a good 'talking to', but these should be the exception rather than the rule. A child who frequently hears negative phrases begins to form a picture of him- or herself based on the negative phrases. Our words and actions shape our children's perception of themselves, and it sticks with them through life. When they grow up, they will still hear these words ringing in their ears: 'Why can't you ever ...?' 'How come you never ...?' 'How many times have I told you?' 'What's wrong with you?' 'Won't you ever learn?' 'I guess you'll never get it right.' When we nag our children, we are taking away moments when we could be encouraging and affirming them.

2. Refusing to listen

Listening often takes more energy than talking, especially active listening. Author Barry St Clair says, 'Nothing frustrates children more than to get a predictable grunt, a pat answer or an inattentive response.'[1] But active listening involves staying quiet long enough to hear your child out, and then looking deeper into what he or she is feeling. When you are listening actively, you don't offer quick solutions or interrupt to offer your analysis of the situation. Parents who don't practise active listening with their children are more interested in being heard and making sure their point is made than they are in listening to their child's heart.

3. *Tearing down*

Many parents are so frustrated with their children that they use phrases like, 'Don't be stupid.' (The child says to himself, 'Mum and Dad wish I wasn't so stupid, they're really disappointed in me.'); or 'You're acting like an idiot.' (The child says to himself, 'Mum and Dad think I'm an idiot so that must be true.'); or 'Can't you ever get anything into your head?' (The child says to himself, 'I must not have the ability to get anything into my head.'). Children's minds are like tape recorders. They record all those negative phrases that we give them, and then play them back throughout their lives. Child psychologist Kevin Leman points out that, 'When a child grows up with less than a good self-image, he or she will be handicapped and possibly emotionally crippled for life.'[2]

We cannot take for granted how important communication is to our children's self-image. When we make these negative withdrawals, we are depleting their source of self-esteem. We can only make up for this depletion by countering with many positive, affirming deposits.

The Proper Ways to Affirm (or, How to Make Effective Deposits)

Deposits must be made many times each day. It is not enough to deposit once a week, because our children are having withdrawals made on their account every day by people all around them. Our world is a negative place and our children come into contact every day with people who have had their own account depleted and are unable to make deposits. They withdraw from our children's account through ridicule and anger, or by encouraging dangerous behaviour and other negative actions. These people have had little affirmation in their lives and do not know how to affirm. Every person that our children come into contact with is either a positive influence or a negative influence; they are either making a deposit into or a withdrawal from the lives of our children.

As parents we must make sure that we keep our children's account full by affirming them in many different ways:

1. Look them in the eye

Many parents are so busy and frazzled that they do not take the time to look at their children when they talk to them. Many children spend their day in front of a computer at school or in front of the television at home, and it does not feel natural to look someone in the eye. But it is important in all types of communication to have eye contact. So make sure you and your child's eyes connect!

2. Call them by name

Names are important. Throughout Scripture, we see evidence of this as God describes a person through the name He gives them: Abram became Abraham which means 'father of many nations'; Jacob became Israel which means 'he struggles with God'; Simon became Peter which means 'the rock'. God has many names that reveal His character: *Yahweh* means 'I AM'; *El Shaddai* means 'God Almighty'; *El Elyon* means 'the Most High God'.

On the day each of our boys was born, I wrote them a letter to explain the significance of their names. We thought carefully before we named our sons and we wanted them to understand that their names were special. Both of those letters were postmarked on their actual birth day and remain sealed to preserve the letter as a permanent record of the process we went through to choose their names. We have talked many times to Jeremiah and Caleb about the significance of their names, and will present the actual letters later at an appropriate time. We have noticed that each boy's name fits his personality perfectly!

Explain to your child the importance of his or her name and why you chose it. Then use that name! No one likes to be called 'hey you'. Many parents only call their children by name when they are angry, and then it is usually their full name! Get into the habit of saying your child's name lovingly when you are communicating.

3. Give a specific compliment/ avoid generic compliments

When people tell me I'm wonderful, it worries me. I don't know what that means; it's too generic. I'm not wonderful at everything, surely they know this. So why would they tell me I'm wonderful without telling me why?

When we tell our children they are great, or fantastic, or special without telling them why, we are making a withdrawal from their account. We have not given them a reason why we think those things about them, and as far as they are concerned, it means nothing. When we tack on the word *because* and then give them a reason, their ears perk up and they listen to what we are saying. 'You are special *because* you are kind to your little brother.' This affirmation gives something for your child to grasp. He now knows one of the reasons why Mum and Dad think he's special. And most importantly, we are making a deposit into their account. We are giving them a specific affirmation that will stay with them throughout life.

Affirm as You Discipline

There will be times when we have to make withdrawals out of our children's account. Times of discipline are inevitable, but if we have been making regular deposits through affirmation and encouragement, they will not be left empty. Children who have not received affirmation and encouragement will rebel when they are disciplined. They have been emptied of self-esteem and self-worth, and many times they turn to the world to search for approval and answers.

When it is time to make a withdrawal through discipline, it is important to remember to do the following four things.

1. Discuss the offence

Talk to your child about the limits that were set in place for a particular offence. For instance, if Johnny stays out beyond the agreed time one evening, he needs to tell you why his actions were wrong. Don't be afraid to have a give-and-take dialogue with your child about why certain rules are in place. The chances are, your child is only testing the waters. He or she is making sure the boundaries are in place.

2. Negotiate the discipline

Talk with your child about what he or she thinks is the appropriate discipline for his or her actions. For many of those actions, the discipline will already have been decided if you have a contract. Before Johnny was allowed to go out at night he knew what his curfew would be, and he knew what the discipline would be if he stayed out past that time. But often we encounter unforeseen situations that require discipline. It is just as important in those instances to allow your children to help negotiate their own discipline. Their idea of discipline may be for you to take away broccoli for a week; your idea of discipline is to beat them within an inch of their life. There should be a balance between those two extremes that you and your children can agree on. Remember, you want your children to have input into the situation, not control of the situation.

3. Carry out the discipline

It is important to follow through with what has been decided by you and your child. If the child has been a part of negotiating his own discipline, he will feel that he has been treated fairly and will understand and accept his discipline. Stephen Glenn says, 'Research shows that children whose parents won't set reasonable limits or who won't follow through on the ones that have been set, believe that their parents do not love them.'[3]

4. Reaffirm our love

This step affirms our children's worth. Children can handle any discipline if they know that there will be a hug or an 'I love you' waiting for them. Dr Kevin Leman talks about the importance of this with regard to spanking. 'The key to follow up ... is physical contact. Hold the child and talk to him about your feelings. Explain what made you angry and why it was necessary to spank. And explain what you expect from the child in the future ... During the "follow-up time", tell him you love him. Explain that there will be times when he will do things that are wrong, but even though he does these things you will never stop loving him and caring about him.'[4]

When Jeremiah was seven and Caleb four, they spent an evening watching a circus performance on the television. They were so impressed by all the stunts and tricks that they decided to try one of their own. I'll never forget what I saw as I came walking into my kitchen that evening. Caleb was sitting against the wall and Jeremiah was poised a few feet in front of him holding a carving knife that was about to go sailing through the air. Caleb was grinning from ear to ear, oblivious to what was about to happen.

Before I could let out a primal parental scream, Jeremiah flung the knife and it hit the kitchen wall just a few inches from Caleb's head. I would like to tell you that I assessed the situation calmly and then sat down with Jeremiah and explained the dangers of flinging sharp kitchen utensils at the heads of family members. That is not what I did. In fact, I don't think I uttered any words as I dragged my eldest son back into his bedroom and put my belt to his bottom. I finally was able to speak, but only to tell him that he wasn't to get up out of his bed until morning.

With the steam still puffing out of my ears, I stomped back into the living room and sat down weakly in a chair. Jeremiah's sniffles could barely be heard in the living room. I blocked them out easily and assured myself that he would fall asleep soon. After a few minutes, the tiny sniffles ascended into a low moaning cry, designed to get my attention. I ignored his crying and turned up the television.

Since the low moaning cry was getting no response, he went on to 'level three', a long high-pitched wail that sounded like it could blow the roof off. The television couldn't drown him out now, but I waited patiently for silence. He would soon cry himself to sleep and the ordeal would be over. I drummed my fingers on the arm of the chair, my patience wearing thin. Unbelievably, the wails grew louder, and I began to worry that one of the neighbours was probably already frantically ringing the police, so I stomped back into his room and flung open the door.

'What is wrong with you?' I bellowed. Jeremiah looked up at me with his red, swollen eyes and wet, messy face and said, 'Dad, you forgot to tell me that you love me after you spanked me.'

My heart sank into my shoes. He wasn't wailing because he had done something wrong, or because I had spanked him. His heart was broken because I didn't take the time, as I normally do, to put my arms around him and remind him that he is still loved. I fell to my knees, hugged him and asked him to forgive me for rushing out of his room before I had done the most important thing: affirmed him by telling him that I loved him, even though I needed to discipline him.

Older children and teenagers also need this assurance. Telling them that we love them and that we believe in them is an important action to take when they have messed up. We need to continually affirm them and let them know that their worth has already been decided. Because God loves them, they are worthy. And because they are our children, we also love them unconditionally.

Allow Your Children to Affirm You!

When I was a youth pastor and my son was in my youth group, I realized something unsettling: my son lived with his youth pastor! I worried about whether this was going to be good for my sons, or whether I should consider giving up my job as a youth pastor now that they were getting older. After fretting over the decision for a while, I decided to talk to Jeremiah.

'Jeremiah,' I said to him one day, 'you're the only one in our youth group who doesn't have a youth pastor. I'm your dad. I'll always be your dad. Every trip we go on, every event we have, your dad will be there. I'm willing to give that up for you guys. I can do something else and allow you to be a part of a youth group without your dad there all the time.'

Jeremiah thought for a moment then said, 'Dad, I don't want you to do that. There's nobody else in this entire world that I would rather have as a youth pastor than you.' During the years my boys were in my youth group, there were no two people who affirmed me more than they did.

Parents, our children need to learn to affirm from our role modelling. And as they learn to give affirmation, allow them to give some to you. We should be role modelling affirmation with each member of our family, and as we do this our children will learn how it is done.

I travel frequently, and my wife affirms me even when I'm gone by leaving little notes all over my suitcase, in my trouser pocket, in my briefcase. When I'm at home, we have 'I love you' days. They aren't planned, but if someone decides that they want a certain day to be an 'I love you' day, they spend the day affirming and telling other family members that they are loved. It's easy to get busy and stressed out in our world, and it's nice to have a family member spending the day reminding everyone that they are loved and appreciated.

Be careful about giving family members insincere praise. Children are excellent at knowing if you are being dishonest with them. If you cannot find anything encouraging to say to your child, don't make up something! Instead, look for little things during the day that you can say to encourage your child. If she is an early riser, say something like, 'I appreciate the way you hop out of bed in the mornings. It makes it easier for our family when you get up and around quickly.' This may seem like a small thing, but you are making a deposit into her account. Even the small encouragements build our children up and make them feel appreciated.

Strong Enough to Withstand the Storms

When we affirm our children, we give them the tools they need to get a grip on living in a tough world. I have seen children whose lives have been shattered by too many negative withdrawals. They walk around with their head down, beaten down emotionally, and desperately searching for approval from anyone. They do not see themselves as God sees them: lovable, precious, and worth dying for. They cannot comprehend that anyone would believe in them that much.

I have also seen children whose accounts are filled with positive deposits from those around them. They are continually affirmed, even when they are disciplined. They are sure of themselves and have the confidence to make their own decisions about what values they will choose. They accept the love of God easily, because they feel that they are worthy of being loved. They are not haughty or full of pride, but secure and stable. They don't spend their days feeling that the world is unfair and unjust.

No one should be a bigger cheerleader for your child than you. Just as you cheered your baby on as he was learning to walk, you should continue to cheer on your thirteen-year-old as he faces the turbulence of adolescence.

When our boys were four and seven we decided that we wanted to develop a tradition in our family. We concluded that we would enter Caleb, Jeremiah and Dad in the Tulsa Run, an annual running event in our town, and race as the 'Moore Boys'. Ten thousand people showed up for this race as contestants. I had not run any appreciable distance since my days in the military. Before the start of the race, I took the boys to the back of the pack and explained to them we would run as far as we (I) could and then walk the rest of the way. Our objective that day was to finish the three mile 'fun run' course, and let the real runners compete in the 10 kilometre run. 'Do you understand?' I asked them. Both little heads bobbed up and down affirmatively.

The gun went off and we just jogged in one place for the first few minutes until the mass of runners moved ahead and we could finally see daylight. I had planned to run straight down the middle of the street because that would be the shortest distance. Things were going well for us. Jeremiah and Caleb were about ten feet in front of me skipping from side to side, having the time of their life. 'How are you all doing?' 'Fine, Dad,' came the reply. Half way through the race I began to feel my heart throb, my breath getting harder and harder to catch. The boys were grabbing street sign poles, spinning themselves in circles waiting for Dad to catch up. 'Caleb, aren't you tired?' I mumbled weakly. Not aware of my 'concern', he waved his little arms motioning for me to catch up with him.

If the first mile and a half was awful, the last part of the race was torture. The course ends with a climb up a long steep hill to Main Street, followed by a right turn on to Main, and on towards the finishing line. We came to the hill and my heart was beating several levels above 'pounding'. I felt my left leg go numb, it felt like a dead stump attached to my hip, and I struggled to drag it along, using the one 'good' leg I had left. Looking ahead, I saw Caleb, still having the time of his life and running as if we had just started. Perhaps, I thought, I could use him for an excuse. 'Caleb, this — is — your — first — race — and — I — think — you — need — a — rest,' I said, gasping for air between each word. 'Come on, Dad,' he said as he was skipping backwards.

Clank, clank, clank. I looked over to my right and saw a lady passing me up the hill. She looked nine months pregnant and was pushing another baby in a pram! I began to pray, 'Lord, if You are going to come back today, and I *really* hope You are ... come quickly!' Finally making it to the top of the hill, we made our right-hand turn, and we were the only runners on the street. Looking over towards the pavement, I saw several of our church members and all I thought about was how embarrassing it would be for me to collapse right in front of them.

Then a voice from the crowd started chanting, 'Caleb, Caleb.' Another voice joined in, 'Caleb, Caleb.' Soon there were a dozen voices, and that turned into several dozen, all chanting his name. Little Caleb raised both arms up in the air and made a victory sign with the fingers on each hand, and began to high-step towards the finishing line. Now a thousand, it seemed, were chanting his name, 'CALEB, CALEB!' Crossing the finishing line, I dropped to the ground, grabbed my chest, and began trying to catch my breath. All of a sudden I felt someone sitting on my heaving chest and he began to cry. Looking up and gasping for oxygen, I said, 'Caleb, what is the matter?' as I felt his tears falling on my face. 'Daddy, didn't you hear them yelling my name? "Caleb, Caleb!"' 'Yes, Caleb, I heard them.' 'Daddy, they want me to run it ONE MORE TIME!'

Your children need to experience the same encouragement. When your children come home from school you ought to be encouraging them. Encourage them in their academic pursuits, their sports activities, in their drama participation. Whatever they are trying to accomplish, encourage them. And encourage them in their spiritual development.

Encourage them to live for Jesus one more day, to make one more lap, when others will try to 'disqualify' them. Each time your child looks into your eyes for approval, they should see it. This does not mean that we are not disappointed in them when they disobey, but your child should know that underneath that disappointment there is unconditional love. Unconditional love doesn't make our children feel that they have to be perfect to win our love. Our love is always there.

As parents, our job is to help our children become all that God wants them to be so that they can be used by Him, for His kingdom. As we continue to affirm our children throughout their lives, we are helping them stand strong against the storms that will inevitably come their way.

When the first phase of your parenting job is through and your children are walking away from you and into the arms of a waiting world, what tools will they take with them? Will you be able to send them away, knowing that you have affirmed their self-worth? If you can say yes, then you can rest assured that your children will be able to tackle even the toughest days with a steadfast belief in themselves.

Thinking It Through

1. Are you comfortable affirming your children, even when they are being disciplined? If not, why not?
2. Is your house filled with more positive words or negative words? How about actions?
3. What deposits are you making each day into the account of your children? What withdrawals are you making?
4. Are you role modelling affirmation in your home with your spouse and children? Do you see your children following your example and affirming other family members?
5. Who is the person who affirmed you the most in your life and how did that make you feel?

Getting a Grip

1. If you have small children, start talking to them at eye level so you can make eye contact. If they are not used to this, they might be uncomfortable at first, but continue the practice until they come to expect it.
2. Write your child a letter, telling him or her why you think he or she is terrific. Give specific examples, not just generic compliments.
3. Practise being a 'high-touch' family by hugging, cuddling and kissing.
4. Get into the habit of affirming your children with words like, 'Good job,' 'Now you've got it!' 'I knew you could do it!'

Did God Fail as a Parent?

Parenting is the toughest job you'll ever have. You can't resign and you never retire. From the day each of our sons was born, Cathy and I have had the responsibility of caring, nurturing, admonishing, disciplining, teaching, serving and understanding them – sometimes all at the same time!

Even after we provided them with a secure home, sent them to good schools, took them to church, and tried to do everything else right, they have still made some wrong choices. Every parent faces this frustration. And many parents have cried out to God, wondering if He understands the hurt.

You Don't Have to Be Perfect to Get the Job Done

One day, as I was pouring my heart out to God, I admitted that I felt like a failure as a parent. As I prayed, a voice inside me said, 'Yes, I understand. I provided My children with everything they needed also. I gave them a nice garden to live in, provided them with food, each other and a beautiful world to enjoy. But it was not enough. They made a wrong choice too.' I smiled. Of course He understood. He was a parent too!

It's a relief to know that I don't have to be a perfect parent. Our children will remember many things about their childhood, but they will forget many things too. If I can do my very best, and still only be consistent 51 per cent of the time, they'll still get the message.

Don't Expect Your Children to Be Perfect

Get ready. Your children are going to make choices you don't agree with. But you can't go out in the world and choose for them, you can only do your best to prepare them for those choices. Many parents think if they make all of their children's choices for them, they are preparing them for the world. But you only prepare them by helping them learn how to choose. When the time comes for your children either to accept or reject Jesus Christ, you can't do it for them. You have to step back and let them choose for themselves.

Life is a learning process and mistakes are part of that process. Our responsibility is to help our children learn from those mistakes.

Give Them Back to God and Then Enjoy Them!

My children were dedicated to God the day they were born. They are His. Many times I have tried to take them back, but He has a firm hold on them! So often we say that our children are dedicated to God, but we act as if we are the only ones working in their lives. Be assured that God is working in your children's lives. But we must continually lift them up in prayer. God has called Christians to establish His kingdom in this world, and my children are a part of that process. Since they belong to God, and they are in His hands, I can learn to enjoy them. I will still worry and fret over them, but I continue to give them back to Him each day to use for His glory.

Be Ready When It Is Time for Them to Go

Our children cannot be our only source of joy. God will not step from His throne and allow our children to take His place. If Jesus is not our foundation, we will crumble. Our children will bring us joyful moments and years of happiness, but they will also disappoint us. They will bring some heartaches and eventually they will leave to begin their own lives.

In the Bible, there is a story of a father who lost it all – his house, his job, his health, his wife and his children. In the world's eyes, he had no reason left to live. After listening to advice from his friends, and even questioning for himself the reasons for his fate, he sat amidst the ruins of his life and uttered these words, 'Though he slay me, yet I will hope in him' (Job 13:15 NIV). Quite simply, Job's life was built on the unfailing promises of a loving God, not upon the things that can vanish in an instant.

Give your children the tools they need to get a grip on life: self-esteem, values and responsibilities, a healthy sexual identity, and good communication. Then release them into the world, knowing that God, the perfect Father, will protect them and use them for the glory of His kingdom!

Pray for Your Children

A fellow minister and friend of mine, Tom Hufty, shared with me one day that he prayed scriptures for his children. I thought it was such a wonderful idea that I wanted to share it with you.

How to Pray Scripture for Your Children

One thing I know for sure about prayer is that when I'm praying scripture, I am praying right. To pray God's Word for your children is a solid means of protecting and providing for them. For when you pray, God can do things that you cannot.

Protection

'But the Lord is faithful, and he will strengthen and protect you from the evil one' (2 Thessalonians 3:3 NIV).

Lord, I pray today that You would continue to be faithful to strengthen and protect _______ from the evil one.

Provision

'But my God shall supply all your need according to his riches in glory by Christ Jesus' (Philippians 4:19).

Lord, I pray today that You would supply all of _______ needs according to Your riches in Christ Jesus.

Holiness

'How can a young man keep his way pure? By living according to your word. I seek you with all my heart; do not let me stray from your commands. I have hidden your word in my heart that I might not sin against you' (Psalm 119:9–11 NIV).

Lord, I ask that _______ will keep pure by keeping Your commands, and taking Your Word to heart.

Blessing

'Oh, that you would bless me and enlarge my territory! Let your hand be with me, and keep me from harm so that I will be free from pain' (1 Chronicles 4:10 NIV).

Lord, I pray that You would do good things for _______ . I pray You will protect _______ from pain and _______ would sense Your presence.

Peers

'Blessed is the man who does not walk in the counsel of the wicked or stand in the way of sinners or sit in the seat of mockers' (Psalm 1:1 NIV).

Lord, I pray _______ will not listen to the counsel of the wicked. I pray _______ will not engage in the behaviour of sinful peers.

Attitude

'... whatever is true, whatever is noble, whatever is right, whatever is pure, whatever is lovely, whatever is admirable – if anything is excellent or praiseworthy – think about such things' (Philippians 4:8 NIV).

Lord, I pray _______ will develop healthy thinking patterns that will be good and worthy of praise. I pray that honest and honourable, right and pure thoughts will dominate ________ days.

We ask these things according to Your Word and in Your Holy Son's name. Amen.

After you have done all that you can, then you trust the scripture, 'Train a child in the way he should go, and when he is old he will not turn from it' (Proverbs 22:6 NIV).

References

Chapter 1

1 Rela M. Geffen et al., *Celebration and Renewal: Rites of Passage in Judaism* (Philadelphia, PA and Jerusalem: The Jewish Publication Society, 1993), 53.

2 Jerry Johnston, *Going All the Way* (Waco, TX: Word Books, 1988), 27.

3 Karen L. Swisher et al., *Teenage Sexuality* (San Diego: Greenhaven Press, Inc., 1994), 72.

4 Geffen et al., 62–63.

5 Ina Corrine Brown, *Understanding Other Cultures* (Englewood Cliffs, NJ: Prentice Hall, Inc., 1963), 55.

Chapter 2

1 Stephen Glenn, *Raising Children for Success* (Fair Oaks, CA: Sunrise Press, 1987), 63.

2 Verne Becker, 'Families: Then and Now," *The Home Survival Guide*, (Internet).

3 Glenn, 91.

4 Kevin Leman, *Making Your Children Mind Without Losing Yours* (New York: Dell Publishing Co., 1984), 63.

5 William Mahedy and Janet Bernardi, *A Generation Alone* (Downers Grove, IL: InterVarsity Press, 1994), 55-56.

6 Glenn, 115.

7 Ibid., 38.

Chapter 3

1 Dr Paul Faulkner, *Raising Faithful Kids in a Fast-Paced World* (West Monroe, LA: Howard Publishing Co., 1995), 18.

2 William J. Bennett, *The De-Valuing of America: The Fight for Our Culture and Our Children* (New York: Summit Books, 1992), 35.

Chapter 5

1 Josh McDowell, *What I Wish My Parents Knew About My Sexuality* (San Bernardino, CA: Here's Life Publishers, 1987), 26–27.
2 Ronald L. Kotesky, *Understanding Adolescence* (Wheaton, IL: Victor Books, 1987), 14–15.
3 Ibid., 12.
4 Ibid., 12–13.
5 Ibid., 12.
6 Grolier's Internet Encyclopedia.
7 Jerry Johnston, *Going All the Way* (Waco, TX: Word Publishers, 1988), 22.

Chapter 6

1 'Sex and America's Teenagers', *Family Planning Perspectives* (The Alan Guttmacher Institute, 1994), 20.
2 Stacy Rinehart and Paula Rinehart, *Choices* (Colorado Springs, CO; NavPress, 1982), 24.
3 Bruce Barton et al., *Life Application Bible* (Wheaton, IL: Tyndale House Publishers, Inc; Grand Rapids, MI: Zondervan Publishing House, 1991), 11.
4 Barry St Clair and Bill Jones, *Sex: Desiring the Best* (San Bernardino: CA: Here's Life Publishers, 1987), 73–74.
5 Barry and Carol St Clair, *Talking With Your Kids About Sex and Dating* (San Bernardino, CA: Here's Life Publishers, 1989), 15.
6 Josh McDowell, *Why Wait: What You Need to Know About the Teen Sexuality Crisis* (San Bernardino, CA: Here's Life Publishers, 1987), 15.

Chapter 7

1 'Talking With Kids About Sex and Sexuality', *Children Now* (Internet).
2 '... Talking About Sex. What the Experts Have to Say', *Jewish Family & Life Magazine* (Internet).
3 Sol Gordon et al., *The Sexual Adolescent: Communicating With Teenagers About Sex* (North Scituate, MA: Druxbury Press, 1979), 8.
4 Josh McDowell, *How to Help Your Child Say No to Sexual Pressure* (Waco, TX: Word Books, 1987), 103.
5. '... Talking About Sex. What the Experts Have to Say', *Jewish Family & Life Magazine* (Internet).
6 'How to Make Talking About Sex Easier for Parents', *Jewish Family & Life Magazine* (Internet).

Chapter 8

1 Stephen Glenn, *Raising Children for Success* (Fair Oaks, CA: Sunrise Press, 1987), 28.

2 Ibid., 26.

3 Paul Faulkner, *Raising Faithful Children in a Fast-Paced World* (West Monroe, LA: Howard Publishing Co., 1995), 154.

4 Jay Kessler, *The Ten Mistakes Parents Make With Teens and How to Avoid Them* (Brentwood, TN: Woglemuth and Hyatt Publishers, Inc., 1988), 66.

Chapter 9

1 Barry St Clair, *Talking With Your Kids About Love, Sex and Dating* (San Bernardino, CA: Here's Life Publishers, 1989), 52.

2 Kevin Leman, *Bringing Up Children Without Tearing Them Down* (Colorado Springs, CO: Focus on the Family Publishers, 1993), 10.

3 Stephen Glenn, *Raising Children for Success* (Fair Oaks, CA: Sunrise Press, 1987), 162.

4 Kevin Leman, *Making Your Children Mind Without Losing Yours* (New York, Dell Publishing Co., 1984), 71–72.

About the Author

Dr Walker Moore is President and Founder of AWE Star Ministries, an organization that is 'raising a generation to reach the globe with the gospel'. As an internationally known conference speaker, he has preached throughout the United States and in many countries such as China, Hungary and Mexico. Dr Moore lives in Tulsa, Oklahoma with his family – wife Cathy and two boys, Jeremiah and Caleb – the joy of his life.

To contact the Author write to:
AWE Star Ministries
P.O. Box 470265
Tulsa, Oklahoma 74147-0265
USA